DICTIONARY
OF TWO-WORD VERBS
FOR STUDENTS OF ENGLISH

EUGENE J. HALL

MINERVA BOOKS, LTD.

30 West 26th Street, New York, NY 10010

Illustrations by Barbara Camhi

Copyright © 1982 by
Eugene J. Hall

Published by
MINERVA BOOKS, LTD.
30 West 26th Street
New York, NY 10010

MANUFACTURED IN THE UNITED STATES OF AMERICA
ISBN: 0-8056-0112-0

INTRODUCTION

Many English verbs are commonly followed by prepositions or adverbs that are understood as part of the verb phrase. Like other verbs, these two-word verbs fall into two classes: transitive — followed by an object — or intransitive — **not** followed by an object. An example of a transitive two-word verb is:

Many people have **given up smoking** in recent years.

And an example of an intransitive two-word verb is:

We have to **get off** here; this is the last stop the bus makes.

Two-word verbs that are transitive can also be divided into two classes: those which are separable — the object can come between the two parts of the verb — or those that are inseparable — the object always follows the two parts of the verb.

Let's use **to give up** again. It's possible to phrase our example sentence in two ways:

Many people have **given up smoking** in recent years.
Many people have **given smoking up** in recent years.

When the object is a noun or noun phrase, it can come either directly after the verb or after the second element in the verb phrase. However, when the object becomes longer — that is, when it has more modifiers — it usually follows the second part of the verb.

On the other hand, when the object is a personal pronoun (**me, them,** etc.), it **must** separate the two parts of the verb.

They've **given it up** because it has been proved harmful to one's health.

3

With many other two-word verbs, the two parts of the verb are inseparable; the object always follows the second word. In many verbs of this type, the preposition that follows the verb makes an intransitive verb transitive. From a strict grammatical point of view, the noun phrase that follows the preposition is the object of the preposition, but for practical purposes, speakers of English ordinarily consider the verb and preposition to be a single unit of meaning.

Let's take the verb **to talk** as an example. Here are some intransitive uses of the verb:

> She was talking while I was reading.
> They were talking so loudly that I couldn't hear you.

To talk is also frequently followed by the prepositions **to** and **about. To** is followed by a noun phrase or pronoun that indicates the person (or sometimes the thing) toward which the talking is directed. **About** is followed by a noun phrase or pronoun that indicates the subject of the talking.

> I was **talking to** the personnel manager.
> We were **talking about** my application for the management training program.

Two-word verbs in this class are inseparable; that is, the verb cannot be separated from its preposition by any other word. Verbs of this kind occur in many other languages besides English. For students of English, the principal difficulty with such verbs is learning which preposition follows which verb. For instance, speakers of Spanish, translating from their own language, often say **to think in** or **on** rather than **to think of** or **about,** which are the equivalent expressions in English.

It should be noted that intransitive two-word verbs are necessarily inseparable since they do not take an object that can come between the two parts of the verb. For example:

> I don't like it when people **drop in** unexpectedly; I prefer to know in advance when they're going to visit.

Many two-word verbs form a single unit of meaning that is often, or even usually, unrelated to the meaning of the two separate parts of the expression. In the example of **to give up** which we we have been using, the meaning is "to stop":

> Many people have **given up smoking** in recent years.
> (They've stopped smoking.)

Furthermore, two-word verbs often have more than one meaning. This is true of **to give up,** which can mean "to yield" or "to surrender" as well as "to stop." For example:

> He **gave up** after the police had cornered him. (He surrendered.)

And that leads to three-word verbs. Intransitive two-word verbs are sometimes followed by a preposition which, again, in effect makes these verb phrases transitive. For instance, **to give up** can be followed by **on:**

> I can't solve this problem; I'm going to **give up on it.**

The parts of three-word verbs cannot be separated.

Many two-word verbs can be used either intransitively or transitively. Sometimes there is a difference of meaning between the intransitive and transitive uses. For example, **to speed up** means "to go faster" when it is used intransitively:

> I can't **speed up;** this is as fast as the car can go.

Used transitively, it means "to make someone or something go faster":

> The efficiency expert is examining our operations to see whether we can **speed up our work.**

In its intransitive use, **to speed up** is of course inseparable, like all other intransitive verbs; but in its transitive use it is separable:

> to speed our work up / to speed it up

Other two-word verbs, however, are inseparable in their transitive uses:

> We have to **get off** at the next stop.
> When you **get off the bus,** go around the corner to the right, and you'll see the museum.

An additional aspect of the two-word verb is that new ones come into use frequently. In many cases they make their way into accepted usage, but in others they disappear as quickly as they have become popular. An example of a two-word verb that has been extremely common in the last few years is **to rip off,** which means "to rob" or "to cheat." It is transitive and separable:

The people in the audience felt that the performers had **ripped them off** by not giving any encores.

Another common current expression is **to luck out,** which means "to achieve success by luck."

I really **lucked out** when I got this job.

To luck out is intransitive and therefore inseparable, but it can be made transitive by adding **on** to form a three-word verb:

I **lucked out on** my new job.

As with all three-word verbs, **to luck out on** is transitive and inseparable.

The dictionary of two-word and three-word verbs that follows gives a definition for each verb or for each different use of each verb. This is followed by an abbreviation which indicates the category into which the verb falls. These abbreviations are:

(I/I) = intransitive and therefore inseparable
(T/I) = transitive and inseparable
(T/S) = transitive and separable

As we have seen, these are the three main categories into which two-word verbs fall. In addition, there are some verbs which are used in more than one class. The abbreviations for these verbs are:

(I/I or T/S) — intransitive and inseparable **or** transitive and separable

For many three-word verbs the third word is given in parentheses — for example, **to carry through (on).** The abbreviation then used is:

(I/I) (T/I)

This means that the two-word verb, **to carry through,** is intransitive and of course inseparable, whereas the three-word verb, **to carry through on,** is transitive and inseparable.

In a few cases, two words or expressions are separated by a diagonal line (/). This may indicate that either of the words may be used interchangeably — **to wander away/off,** for example. Or it may indicate that the two words are opposites — **to sign in/out,** for example.

An example of the use of each verb follows. The examples present the verb within a context which should make both the meaning of the verb and the way in which it is used easier to understand. The verbs which have been included are used by educated native speakers of English, both in speech and in writing.

Indeed two-word and three-word verbs are a basic feature of English. The student of English must learn to understand and to use them. This book is offered in the hope that it will make that task easier.

a

to add up

to add, to total (T/S)

I've just *added up all these figures*. I had to *add them up* because I was trying to balance my checkbook, and I needed to find out how much money I'd spent.

to ask over

to invite to visit (T/S)

I'm going to invite Paul and Ginny to the party. I want to *ask them over* because they're so much fun.

b

to back down

to withdraw a claim (I/I)

He was telling a lot of stories about the things he'd done, but when he couldn't show any evidence for them, he had to *back down*.

to back out

to withdraw from an engagement, promise, or undertaking (I/I)

She'd accepted an invitation to the party, but she didn't want to go, so she was looking for an excuse that would let her *back out* gracefully.

to back up

(1) *to go in reverse* (I/I)

You're going to have to *back up* to get the car out of the garage.

(2) *to cause to go in reverse* (T/S)

You can't get out of this street if you don't *back up the car*. You have to *back it up* and then turn to the right.

(3) *to support a claim* (T/S)

The company can *back up all its advertising claims*. It can *back them up* with scientific evidence.

to bang up
to damage   *(T/S)*
The accident wasn't too bad, but I *banged up the left front fender* of my car. I *banged it up* badly enough so that I had to take the car to a body shop for repairs.

to bear down
to press, to make an effort   *(I/I)*
You really aren't making enough of an effort. You'll have to *bear down* if you want to succeed.

to bear down on
(1) *to put pressure on*   *(T/I)*
They've been *bearing down on everybody* in the company. They're putting pressure on them to produce more.

(2) *to come near, to approach*   *(T/I)*
The truck was already *bearing down on me* before I even saw it.

to bear on
to relate to   *(T/I)*
She had a lot to say, but none of it *bore on the problem* that we'd been discussing.

to bear out
to support, to confirm   *(T/S)*
His previous employers didn't *bear out his claims* that he had managerial experience. If they had *borne him out*, we would have hired him.

to bear up (under)
to endure   *(I/I) (T/I)*
We're going to have some bad times ahead. We'll just have to *bear up*. A lot of people find that they can't *bear up under the pressures* of the modern business world.

to bear with
to endure patiently, to tolerate   *(T/I)*
You'll have to *bear with me* if I sound a little confused. I'm still trying to get all the facts straight in my mind.

to beat back

to cause to retreat (T/S)

The enemy attacked us, but we *beat back their forces*. We *beat them back* after an hour of hard fighting.

to beat down

to end or suppress opposition, to make someone yield

(T/S)

She *beat down all the opposition* to her plan. She *beat it down* with her superior reasoning.

to beat off

to make withdraw, to repel (T/S)

The enemy attacked over and over again, but we *beat them off* every time, and they finally withdrew from the field of battle.

to beat up

to give a thorough beating to (T/S)

The robbers said they were going to *beat up my friend*, but before they *beat him up* I was able to get help.

to beg off

to excuse oneself from an engagement, etc. (I/I)

I'd really like to go to your party, but I'm going to have to *beg off*. My parents just called to say that they'd be in town that day.

to block in/out

to outline, to state something in a general way without giving details (T/S)

I'm just *blocking in some rough ideas* now. When I've *blocked them out*, I'll show you what I have in mind, and we can begin to discuss the details.

to block out

to prevent from seeing, to fail to see (T/S)

She's *blocked out the unpleasant things* that have happened to her. She *blocks them out* by remembering only the happy things.

to blow out

(1) *to burst or explode* (I/I)

Luckily I was driving slowly when the tire *blew out*.

(2) *to extinguish by blowing* (T/S)

Please *blow out the candles*. If you don't *blow them out*, you'll get wax all over the table.

to blow over

to pass, to be forgotten (I/I)

The storm *blew over* without causing any damage.

to blow up

(1) *to explode* (I/I)

You have to handle this chemical carefully or else it will *blow up*.

(2) *to make explode* (T/S)

They want to *blow up this building* immediately. Please leave the area before they *blow it up*.

(3) *to lose one's temper* (I/I)

You won't like what I'm going to tell you, but please don't *blow up*. It won't help for you to get angry.

to break down

(1) *to stop working* (I/I)

If your car *breaks down* on the highway, you can get emergency repair service.

(2) *to lose control over one's emotions* (I/I)

When things go wrong, it doesn't help to *break down* and begin to cry.

(3) *to analyze, to separate into parts* (T/S)

They *break down the budget* according to the different parts of the company. They have to *break it down* to find out which divisions are profitable and which are not.

to break in (on)

(1) *to interrupt* (I/I) (T/I)

She *broke in* with what she had to say before I'd finished speaking. She always *breaks in on our discussions*, even though they don't really concern her.

(2) *to train, to accustom to a new routine*   (T/S)
They're going to start *breaking in the new employees* next
week. They'll *break them in* with a special training program.

(3) *to enter by force*   (I/I)
They're installing an alarm system because they're afraid
burglars may *break in.*

to break into
to enter by force   (T/I)
They didn't get an alarm system until burglars had already
broken into the house.

to break off
to stop suddenly   (T/S)
We *broke off our conversation* when he entered the room.
We had to *break it off* because we'd been talking about him.

to break out
(1) *to escape*   (I/I)
All the prisoners were thinking only of *breaking out.* Each
of them had his own escape plan.

(2) *to begin suddenly*   (I/I)
She was so happy that she *broke out* into song.

to break up
(1) *to end a relationship*   (I/I)
Sylvia and Max have been together for a long time, but I
heard just recently that they've *broken up.*

(2) *to put an end to*   (T/S)
They called in the police to *break up the riot.* They finally
broke it up by using tear gas.

(3) *to separate, to break into pieces, to take apart*   (T/S)
They're *breaking up the old cars.* After they've *broken them
up,* they'll sell the parts separately.

to break with
to end a relationship   (T/I)
I don't know what made him *break with his company.*
Maybe he just got tired of the work he was doing and
decided to quit.

to bring about
to cause to happen (T/S)
We have to *bring about some changes* in attitudes, but we can't *bring them about* just by talking. We're going to have to fire those workers who refuse to change.

to bring around
to persuade, to make (someone) change an opinion (T/S)
We have to *bring around the directors* to our way of thinking, but I'm sure we can *bring them around* by presenting them with all the facts and figures.

to bring in
to attract, to produce more business, income, etc. (T/S)
The store is always trying to *bring in more customers*. The best way to *bring them in* is by having a lot of sales.

to bring off
to succeed in (T/S)
I didn't think she could *bring off her new role*, but she managed to *bring it off* because of the brilliance of her acting.

to bring on
to make begin (T/S)
All that noise is going to *bring on one of my headaches*. Noise always *brings them on*.

to bring out
(1) *to issue to the public* (T/S)
She *brings out two books* every year because she's so popular with her readers. She *brings one out* in the spring and another in the fall.

(2) *to show, to reveal* (T/S)
The editors of the newspaper are trying to *bring out the truth* of the matter, but the politicians won't let them *bring it out*.

to bring to
to revive, to bring to consciousness (T/S)
It took a long time to *bring him to* after he'd been hit on the head.

to bring up

(1) *to raise, to rear* *(T/S)*
They *brought up their children* in a small town. They thought it was a healthier environment in which to *bring them up.*

(2) *to mention, to call to one's attention* *(T/S)*
She keeps on *bringing up a lot of things* that I'd rather forget, and it makes me angry whenever she *brings them up.*

to brush off

to dismiss without thought or courtesy *(T/S)*
He's always trying to *brush off his problems* as though they didn't exist. He thinks he can *brush them off* just by ignoring them.

to brush up on

to improve one's memory about something *(T/I)*
I really don't remember much about math. I'll have to *brush up on it* before my children start studying it in school.

to build up

(1) *to increase* *(T/S)*
We want to *build up our sales,* and we think we can *build them up* by doing more advertising.

(2) *to improve in health, strength, etc.* *(T/S)*
He's *building himself up* by exercising an hour every day.

to burn down

(1) *to burn to the ground* *(I/I)*
The building *burned down* because the fire fighters didn't get there fast enough.

(2) *to cause to burn to the ground* *(T/S)*
They wanted to *burn down the building* because by *burning it down* they could collect the insurance money.

to burn up

(1) *to burn completely* *(I/I)*
This paper is so wet it won't *burn up.*

(2) *to cause to burn completely* (T/S)

I was trying to *burn up the paper.* I wanted to *burn it up* so that nobody could see what was written on it.

to burst into/to burst in on

to enter or interrupt abruptly or violently (T/I)

First he *burst into the room* without warning, and then he *burst in on our conversation* without even greeting us.

to burst out

to speak suddenly or violently (I/I)

We asked her to keep our engagement a secret, but she *burst out* with the news one day, so now everybody knows about it.

to buy off

to bribe (T/S)

He's trying to *buy off a lot of politicians* by offering them large sums of money, but he'll find it's impossible to *buy them off.*

to buy out

to buy someone's share in something (T/S)

She wants to *buy out her partners* in the business. After she *buys them out,* she'll control every aspect of the business herself.

to buy up

to buy the entire supply of something (T/S)

The government tried to *buy up all the copper* it could. They wanted to *buy it up* because it was getting scarce.

C

to call down

to scold (T/S)

His supervisor has *called him down* several times because he isn't careful enough.

to call for

(1) *to require* (T/I)

The plan *calls for exact timing.* If things aren't done on schedule, the whole plan will fail.

(2) *to come and get*   *(T/I)*
She said she was going to *call for me* on her way to work, but she hasn't arrived yet.

to call off
to cancel   *(T/S)*
They *called off the meeting* at the last minute. They had to *call it off* because the accountant hadn't submitted the budget yet.

to call on
(1) *to ask to speak*   *(T/I)*
Whenever the teacher *calls on me*, he takes me by surprise, and I can't get a word out.

(2) *to visit*   *(T/I)*
I'm going to *call on all my old friends* when I go back to my hometown this summer.

to call up
(1) *to telephone*   *(I/I or T/S)*
She never *calls up*, so I keep *calling her up*, but no one answers the phone.

(2) *to call for military service*   *(T/S)*
The government is considering *calling up young men and women* for military service. They may start to *call them up* next year.

(3) *to bring to mind*   *(T/S)*
These pictures *call up some very pleasant memories* of my vacation. They'll keep *calling them up* for a long time.

to calm down
(1) *to become calm or quiet*   *(I/I)*
You shouldn't get so excited. You have to learn to *calm down*.

(2) *to make calm or quiet*   *(T/S)*
They were having a terrible fight, but I managed to *calm them down*.

She can't always give the older children all the attention they want because she has to *care for the baby*.

to care for
    (1) *to like*   *(T/I)*
She's never *cared for office work*. She's never liked it, and she isn't going to start liking it now.

    (2) *to look after, to tend*   *(T/I)*
She can't always give the older children all the attention they want because she has to *care for the baby*.

to carry away
    to overcome with emotion   *(T/S)*
I'm sorry I'm crying. The sound of the national anthem always *carries me away*.

to carry off
    (1) *to remove*   *(T/S)*
Those men just *carried off my desk*. Why did they *carry it off?*

    (2) *to succeed in a difficult situation*   *(T/S)*
I didn't think she'd be able to persuade the directors to accept her plan, but she managed to *carry it off* because she gave them such excellent reasons.

to carry on
    (1) *to continue*   *(I/I)*
I know things are difficult right now, but you'll just have to *carry on* until they get better.

    (2) *to do, to perform*   *(T/S)*
You can't *carry on your personal activities* at work. You should *carry them on* during your leisure time.

to carry out
    to put into effect, to accomplish   *(T/S)*
The employees aren't really ready to *carry out the new procedures*. They'll need special training before they can *carry them out*.

to carry over
    to continue at a later time or a different place   *(T/S)*
They didn't have to cover all the items on the agenda, so they've *carried some of them over* until the meeting next week.

to carry through (on)

to get done, to accomplish   *(I/I) (T/I)*

You never finish anything. You have to learn to *carry through*. Your friend keeps on getting promoted because she *carries through on every job* they give her.

to catch at

to reach for, to try to seize   *(T/I)*

He isn't an original thinker, so he's always *catching at other people's ideas.*

to catch on

(1) *to understand*   *(I/I)*

It took me a long time to *catch on*, but when I finally did understand what he was saying, it all made sense to me.

(2) *to become fashionable*   *(I/I)*

Pocket calculators have really *caught on*. Just about everyone you see has one nowadays.

to catch up

to come from behind   *(I/I)*

I'm trying to *catch up*, but they've given me so much work that it's going to take a long time.

to catch up on

to become current with   *(T/I)*

I was sick for several days, so now I'm working late to *catch up on all the work* that piled up while I was away from the office.

to catch up with

to overtake   *(T/I)*

He works hard because he feels he has *to catch up with the other people* in the office. He doesn't have as much education as they do.

to check in

to arrive, to register   *(I/I)*

You have to sign the register when you *check in* at a hotel.

to check off
> *to mark something as being finished or examined*   *(T/S)*
> He stands there with a clipboard and *checks off each item* as it comes off the assembly line. After he *checks one off,* he examines the next one.

to check out (of)
> *to leave*   *(I/I)* *(T/I)*
> You have to pay your bill when you *check out of a hotel.* Sometimes there's a long line when you want to *check out.*

to check up on
> *to investigate, to examine*   *(T/I)*
> I want you to *check up on these figures.* They don't look right to me, and I want to see if there's an error in them. After you *check up on them* let me know what you find.

to cheer up
> (1) *to become cheerful or happy*   *(I/I)*
> I don't seem to be able *to cheer up* today. Everything seems pretty bad to me.
>
> (2) *to make cheerful or happy*   *(T/S)*
> I tried to *cheer up my sister* by telling her a lot of jokes, but nothing I said could *cheer her up.*

to chew up
> *to chew thoroughly*   *(T/S)*
> You should *chew up every mouthful of food.* You should *chew it up* thoroughly before you try to swallow it.

to chip in
> *to contribute money or help*   *(I/I or T/S)*
> They're always asking us to *chip in a few dollars* for this or that at the office. The last time they asked me, I didn't have any money, so I couldn't *chip in.*

to chop down
> *to cut down a tree, etc., with an axe*   *(T/S)*
> The people protested when the city tried to *chop down some trees.* They said they wanted to preserve them rather than *chop them down.*

21

to chop up
  to chop (cut with an axe) into pieces   (T/S)
  He's out *chopping up the wood* now. The logs were too big
  for the fireplace, but after he's *chopped them up*, we can
  have a nice fire.

to clean off
  to clean the surface of   (T/S)
  When are you going to *clean off your desk?* If you *cleaned
  it off*, you could do your work more efficiently.

to clean out
  to empty   (T/S)
  I thought I'd *cleaned out all the drawers* in my desk, but
  even after I'd *cleaned them out*, my wife found some things
  I'd overlooked.

to clean up
  (1) *to clean, to clean thoroughly*   (I/I)
  I *cleaned up* after work because I had a big date for the
  evening, and I wanted to look my best.

  (2) *to clean, to clean thoroughly*   (T/S)
  I always *clean up the house* on Saturday. After I've *cleaned
  it up*, I usually ask some friends over.

  (3) *to finish*   (T/S)
  I'm going to *clean up this job* on Friday. After I've *cleaned
  it up*, I'll take a few days off.

to clear away
  to remove   (T/S)
  The busboy is *clearing away the dirty dishes*. After he's
  cleared them away, he'll set the table again.

to clear off
  to clear the surface, to get rid of objects on the surface
                                                             (T/S)
  Yes, I *clear off my desk* every night. I *clear it off* by throwing everything in the wastebasket.

to clear out
   to empty   *(T/S)*
   I haven't *cleared out my in-basket* yet. I have to answer
   two or three more letters before I can *clear it out*.

to clear out (of)
   to leave   *(I/I) (T/I)*
   Everybody had *cleared out of the room* before the bell rang.
   I've never seen the students in such a hurry to *clear out*.

to clear up
   (1) *to become clear, speaking of the weather*   *(I/I)*
   Look! There's some blue sky over there! I thing it's going
   to *clear up* in an hour or so.

   (2) *to make clear, comprehensible*   *(T/S)*
   I hope my explanation has *cleared up the problem* for you.
   If I haven't *cleared it up*, I'll try to explain it again.

   (3) *to heal, especially a skin condition*   *(T/S)*
   This medicine should *clear up that rash* of yours. If it
   hasn't *cleared it up* in a few days, we'll try something
   stronger.

to close down
   to shut completely or permanently   *(I/I or T/S)*
   They're talking about *closing down the factory*. They say
   they have to *close it down* because it's no longer a profitable enterprise, but I don't know what I'll do if it does
   close down.

to close in (on)
   to approach and surround in a threatening manner
                                                          (I/I) (T/I)
   They were very frightened when they saw the mob *closing
   in*. They weren't sure they'd be able to escape if the mob
   closed in on them any further.

to close out
   to end, to get rid of all of a product   *(T/S)*
   We're having a big sale on these items because we're *closing out this line of goods*. After we've *closed it out*, we
   don't plan to carry this type of merchandise any more.

to close up
to close or shut, often for a short period of time
(I/I or T/S)
I got to the store just before it *closed up*. They *close it up* at nine every evening.

to cloud up
to become cloudy   *(I/I)*
It was clear a while ago, but it's beginning to *cloud up* now. You can only see a bit of blue sky.

to come about
to happen   *(I/I)*
I don't know how it *came about* or who was responsible for it, but I was certainly glad when I got my promotion.

to come across
to find by accident   *(T/I)*
I'd been looking for this book for a long time, and I finally *came across it* in the most unexpected place.

to come along (with)
to make progress   *(I/I) (T/I)*
The report is finally *coming along* all right, but I wasn't *coming along with it* too well until I got all the facts and figures.

to come along with
to accompany   *(T/I)*
I want you to *come along with me* when I go to get my driver's license. I'm nervous about the test, and I'd like to have someone with me.

to come by
to visit   *(I/I)*
I wasn't expecting to see her, so I was very happy when she *came by* for a few minutes on her way to the airport.

to come down with
to catch an illness   *(T/I)*
I can't go to work today because I've *come down with a terrible cold*.

I'd been looking for this book for a long time, and I finally *came across it* in the most unexpected place.

25

to come in

to enter   *(I/I)*

We were standing on the steps outside the school when the teacher called to us to *come in*. It was time for the class to begin.

to come into

to inherit   *(T/I)*

They're very wealthy, but not because of their own efforts. They *came into their money* by inheritance.

to come out

(1) *to come to an end*   *(I/I)*

I never found out how the story *came out* because I didn't have time to finish reading it.

(2) *to be revealed*   *(I/I)*

The truth of the matter *came out* even though they had tried to hide it.

to come out with

to say something unexpected   *(T/I)*

She's always *coming out with something funny*. You can never tell what she's going to say next, but you can be sure that it will make you laugh.

to come over

to come to another place   *(I/I)*

I'd rather you *came over* here because it's too difficult for me to get to your house.

to come through

to achieve success in spite of difficulties   *(T/I)*

We had a lot of problems getting our business started, but we *came through them all*, and now the business is a great success.

to come through (with)

to perform a desired action   *(I/I) (T/I)*

He was very unhappy because management didn't *come through with the promotion* he'd been expecting. This is the second time they haven't *come through*, and he says if it happens again, he'll quit.

to come to

(1) *to recover consciousness* *(I/I)*
I was unconscious for a long time after I got hit on the head. It took several minutes before I *came to*.

(2) *to reach, to add up to, to total* *(T/I)*
The bill *came to a lot more* than I expected, but luckily I had enough money with me to pay it.

to come under

(1) *to be under the authority or control of* *(T/I)*
The accounts payable section *comes under the comptroller's office*.

(2) *to fall into a group or category* *(T/I)*
All these books should *come under the general heading* of sociology.

to come up

to arise by chance in a discussion *(I/I)*
I don't know exactly how the subject *came up*; we were talking, and someone just happened to mention it.

to come up to

to be equal to *(T/I)*
They've given her a lot of new responsibilities because they think she'll *come up to them* easily.

to come up with

to propose, to state an idea *(T/I)*
He's the idea man at the advertising agency. He's always *coming up with new concepts* that will catch the eye of the public.

to cook up

to scheme, to devise a scheme *(I/I or T/S)*
I don't know what kind of scheme he's *cooked up* now. When he does *cook something up*, it will probably be fantastic.

to cool down/off

(1) *to become cool* *(I/I)*
The coffee is still too hot; I can't drink it until it *cools off*.

27

(2) *to make cool* (T/S)

If you put some milk in your coffee, the milk will *cool it down.*

(3) *to recover one's temper* (I/I)

Just *cool down* now. You'll never make any friends if you keep getting angry with people all the time.

to copy out

to copy in full, to copy by hand (T/S)

Before printing was discovered, scribes had to *copy out books* by hand. If often took months to *copy one out.*

to count in

to include (T/S)

Yes, I want to join the club. Please *count me in.*

to count on/upon

to rely on (T/I)

You shouldn't *count on me* to be there. I have a lot of other things to do that week, so I don't know whether or not I'll be able to attend.

to count out

to exclude (T/S)

That scheme of yours doesn't sound legal to me. I don't want any part of it. Just *count me out.*

to count up

to count, to total (T/S)

We haven't *counted up all the accounts receivable.* When we do *count them up,* we expect that they'll amount to a considerable sum of money.

to cover up

to hide, to conceal (T/S)

They tried to *cover up the scandal,* but they couldn't *cover it up* after some reporters heard some rumors about it.

to crack down

to be strict (I/I)

You've got to *crack down.* If you don't, you won't have any discipline in your class.

to crack down on
to be strict with or about   *(T/I)*
They're *cracking down on the employees* to make them report to work on time.

to crack up
to break down emotionally   *(I/I)*
He's afraid he's going to *crack up* and have a real nervous breakdown if they keep on loading him down with more work.

to creep up (on)
to approach silently, stealthily   *(I/I) (T/I)*
Don't *creep up* that way. I didn't hear you coming, and it startled me. I don't like it when you *creep up on me.*

to cross off/out
to remove (as from a list)   *(T/S)*
She found out that they'd *crossed off her name* from the list of promotions, but she hasn't found out why they *crossed it out.*

to cry out
to cry, to shout   *(I/I)*
What was that terrible sound? I'm sure I heard someone *cry out!*

to cut back (on)
to reduce   *(I/I) (T/I)*
We have to *cut back on our consumption* of gasoline. We can *cut back* by driving less and by using less electricity.

to cut down
to reduce   *(T/S)*
They've *cut down their production* of big cars. They had to *cut it down* because the big cars weren't selling well any more.

to cut down (on)
to reduce   *(I/I) (T/I)*
I'm going to *cut down on eating* things with sugar in them. Do you think I'll lose some weight if I *cut down?*

to cut in (on)

to interrupt   *(I/I) (T/I)*
Don't *cut in* while other people are talking. Let them finish what they have to say. It isn't polite to *cut in on other people's remarks.*

to cut off

(1) *to sever, to amputate*   *(T/S)*
His leg is so badly injured that the doctors don't think they'll be able to save it. They may have to *cut it off.*

(2) *to interrupt, to stop suddenly*   *(T/S)*
First the repairman had to *cut off the electricity.* After he had *cut it off,* he was able to work on the air conditioner.

to cut out

(1) *to eliminate, to remove*   *(T/S)*
She was upset because the editor had *cut out part* of her story. He said that he *cut it out* because he didn't have enough space to print all of it.

(2) *to stop*   *(T/S)*
Cut out all that noise! Just *cut it out!*

to cut up

(1) *to cut in small pieces*   *(T/S)*
She's *cutting up a lot of vegetables.* She's *cutting them up* for the new dish she's making for dinner.

(2) *to behave in a way that attracts attention*   *(I/I)*
That child is always *cutting up.* He does all those terrible things just so that people will notice him.

d

to die away

to fade or stop gradually   *(I/I)*
As we sat on the porch, the light *died away* little by little until it became dark enough for us to see the stars.

to die down

to stop gradually (I/I)

We had a good fire going but it began to *die down* after a while. It was almost out by the time we went to bed.

to die off/out

to go out of existence, to become extinct (I/I)

Many species of both plants and animals have begun to *die off* because they can't compete in an environment which is increasingly controlled for the benefit of human beings.

to dig in

to begin to work hard (I/I)

There was so much work piled up on my desk that I didn't know where to start. I just *dug in* and kept on working until I'd finished it all.

to dig into

to investigate (T/I)

If you really *dig into this material*, you'll be able to find some interesting information for your research project.

to dig out

to get information, to find (T/S)

There's so much to go through that I can't *dig out all the information* now. I'll come back and *dig it all out* tomorrow.

to dig up

(1) *to dig, to excavate, to unearth* (T/S)

The dog has *dug up the flowers* again. He keeps on *digging them up* because he's looking for the bones that he buried in the flower beds.

(2) *to bring to attention anew* (T/S)

I wish they wouldn't *dig up that old scandal*. Every time they *dig it up*, I have to deny that I had anything to do with it.

to dip into

to read at random (T/I)

I've *dipped into the book* here and there, but I haven't tried to sit down and read it from beginning to end.

31

to divide up

to divide   (T/S)

We have to *divide up our duties.* If we don't *divide them up* fairly, some of us will have more work than others.

to do away with

to get rid of, to eliminate   (T/I)

I wish we could *do away with some of this paperwork;* it takes too much time and effort.

to do over

to do again   (T/S)

I have to *do over my homework.* After I *do it over,* there won't be any mistakes in it.

to do without

to get·along without   (T/I)

It's better to *do without sugar* completely than to eat too much of it.

to double back

to return the way one has come   (I/I)

We were sure that we had taken a wrong turn, but when we tried to *double back,* we got completely lost.

to double up

to share with someone   (I/I)

We're so short of space that we've had to *double up* in every office.

to drag on

to continue in a boring way for a long time   (I/I)

The party *dragged on* until the early hours of the morning, even though everyone was tired and wanted to go home.

to drag out

to make continue in a boring way for a long time

          (T/S)

The boss *dragged out the meeting* so long that everybody was yawning. No one understood why he wanted to *drag it out* like that.

to draw on
> *to use to advantage*   *(T/I)*
> When she writes, she *draws on all the information* that she's acquired through years of reading.

to draw out
> *to get someone to talk*   *(T/S)*
> She's really good at *drawing out the people* she meets. She *draws them out* by being interested in the things that interest them.

to draw up
> *to draft or compose a document*   *(T/S)*
> You'll have to get a lawyer to *draw up the affidavit*. If you try to *draw it up* yourself, you'll get it all wrong.

to dream up
> *to devise, to produce*   *(T/S)*
> How do you suppose she *dreams up all those wonderful ideas?* She must have a terrific imagination to be able to *dream them up*.

to dress down
> *to reprimand, to scold*   *(T/S)*
> The supervisor *dressed down* the entire office staff. She *dressed us down* because we hadn't followed the safety regulations for the new machines.

to dress up
> *to put on or wear formal or fancy clothes*   *(I/I)*
> They like to go to parties where they can *dress up* in their best clothes.

to drink in
> *to absorb through the senses or feelings*   *(T/S)*
> We sat for a long time and *drank in the beauty* of the sunset. We wanted to *drink it all in* one last time because our vacation was ending in the morning.

to drink up
> *to drink all of something*   *(I/I or T/S)*
> The children haven't *drunk up all their milk,* and I want them to *drink it all up*. We can't leave until they *drink up*.

to drive at
to mean, to intend to say (T/I)
I don't understand what you're *driving at*. What are you trying to say?

to drop by
to visit for a brief time (I/I)
I have something I want to show you. I'll *drop by* for a minute or two later today, if you don't mind.

to drop in
to visit unexpectedly (I/I)
All these people just *dropped in*. I didn't know any of them were going to visit me.

to drop off
(1) *to leave something somewhere* (T/S)
Can I *drop off these packages* while I'm out doing errands this morning? If you won't be home, I'll *drop them off* tomorrow.

(2) *to fall asleep* (I/I)
I *dropped off* while I was watching TV. I just couldn't keep my eyes open.

to drop out
to quit (I/I or T/I)
You shouldn't *drop out of school*. If you *drop out* now, you may have a hard time getting a job.

to drown out
to make a sound inaudible by making a loud noise (T/S)
The music *drowned out her screams*. If it hadn't *drowned them out*, we would have been able to help her.

e

to eat up
to eat all of something (T/S)
The electricity has gone off, so we're trying to *eat up all the food* in the refrigerator. If we don't *eat it up*, it will spoil.

All these people just *dropped in*. I didn't know any of them were going to visit me.

to end up
  to finish   *(I/I)*
  If you don't learn some special skills, you'll *end up* as just
  another clerk.

to explain away
  to find reasons, to justify   *(T/S)*
  I tried to *explain away the discrepancies* in the figures, but
  I found I couldn't *explain all of them away.*

f

to face up (to)
  to accept as real   *(I/I) (T/I)*
  She just won't *face up to her problems.* If she can't bring
  herself to *face up,* she's never going to be able to improve
  her life.

to fail out (of)
  to fail   *(I/I) (T/I)*
  If you don't study, you'll *fail out,* and if you *fail out of
  school* now, it will end your chances for a good career.

to fall back on/upon
  to turn to for help   *(T/I)*
  She's trying to get a job, but she can't *fall back on the
  experience* she had twenty years ago.

to fall behind (in)
  to fail to keep current   *(I/I) (T/I)*
  Look at all these papers on your desk! Why do you keep
  falling behind in your work all the time? If you *fall behind* any further, you'll never get caught up.

to fall for
  (1) *to fall in love*   *(T/I)*
  The first time we met, I *fell for her.* I knew that this time
  I was really in love.

  (2) *to be deceived by*   *(T/I)*
  He *falls for every scheme* that anyone tells him about. He
  can't tell the difference between honest and dishonest
  people.

to fall off

to become less or smaller   *(I/I)*
Our orders have really started to *fall off*. We haven't been getting nearly as many since our competitors started advertising so heavily.

to fall out (with)

to quarrel (with)   *(I/I) (T/I)*
He's *fallen out with all his old friends*. I don't understand why he keeps on quarreling with them all the time.

to fall through

to fail, to come to nothing   *(I/I)*
All my plans for the party *fell through*. A lot of my friends were busy, and some of the others weren't interested, so I decided to call it off.

to feel out

to get the opinions of someone else   *(T/S)*
He wanted to *feel out the voters* before he decided to become a candidate. Now that he's *felt them out*, he thinks he may have a chance to win the election.

to feel up to

to feel able to do something   *(T/I)*
She's quite sick today. She certainly doesn't *feel up to going* to work.

to fight off

to try to prevent   *(T/S)*
I've been *fighting off a cold*. I've felt that I was coming down with one all week, but so far I've been able to *fight it off*.

to figure on

to count on, to expect   *(T/I)*
My budget is in a mess. I was *figuring on a raise,* and when it didn't come through, I found I'd spent more money than I should have.

to figure out

to understand, to solve, to deduce (T/S)
I had to get some help in *figuring out the math problems.*
I'm not very good in math, so I couldn't *figure them out*
on my own.

to fill in

to complete a form, etc. (T/S)
Fill in every blank on this application form. You have to
fill all of them in or we won't even consider your application.

to fill in (for)

to take the place (of) (I/I) (T/I)
He knows every job in the plant, so we're going to have
him *fill in for the absentee workers.* We need someone
reliable to *fill in* when workers don't show up.

to fill (someone) in on

to give information about (T/I)
I only know the broad outlines of the project, but they'll
fill me in on the details at the meeting on Tuesday.

to fill out

to complete a form, etc. (T/S)
You haven't *filled out your tax return* correctly. You'll
have to *fill it out* again.

to fill up

to fill to the top, to fill completely (T/S)
She *filled up my in-basket* with a week's work. Then after
she'd *filled it up* to the top, she told me I had to finish all
that work in one day.

to find out

to learn, to discover (T/S)
The newspapers are trying to *find out the truth* about the
matter. After they *find it out,* there will probably be a big
scandal.

to finish up

to finish, to finish completely *(I/I or T/S)*

I'm just *finishing up*. I'll come to lunch with you as soon as I *finish up this work*. I can't really enjoy myself until I *finish it up*.

to finish with

to end a relationship with *(T/I)*

I'm *finished with those people.* I don't want to have any more to do with them because they never keep their promises.

to fit in

to make time for *(T/S)*

I'd like to *fit in an appointment* with the dentist today. Will you check his schedule and see if he can *fit me in* sometime this afternoon?

to fit in (with)

to be suited or adjusted (to) *(I/I) (T/S)*

She doesn't *fit in* here. I don't really understand why she hasn't been able to *fit in with the other members* of the staff. She doesn't seem to be able to get along with them.

to fix up

to fix, to repair, to put in order *(T/S)*

I have to *fix up my garden*. The storm caused so much damage that it'll take me a couple of days to *fix it all up*.

to follow through

to complete *(I/I)*

It's no good just to start a job; you have to *follow through* until it's finished correctly.

to follow up (on)

to carry out, to carry toward completion *(I/I) (T/I)*

We have some good prospects for sales, but we have to *follow up*. We'll lose these opportunities if we don't *follow up on them.*

to freeze out
to exclude   (T/S)
He wanted to join the club, but they *froze him out*. They treated him so coldly that he was convinced that they disliked him.

to freeze over/up
to freeze, to become icy   (I/I)
It was so cold last winter that the river *froze over* completely.

to frighten away/off
to make leave out of fear   (T/S)
The dogs barked so much that they *frightened the burglar away*.

g

to get across
to convey an idea, to make understand   (T/S)
He has trouble when he tries to explain things; he often can't *get his ideas across* so that other people can understand them.

to get ahead
to advance, to progress   (I/I)
She works hard because she wants to *get ahead*. She wants to be a big success.

to get ahead (of)
to achieve success, to be in advance (of)   (I/I) (T/I)
He wants to *get ahead*. He's so competitive that he's always trying to *get ahead of everyone else*.

to get along (with)
to be friends (with), to agree (with)   (I/I) (T/I)
I don't know why I can't *get along with her*. We try to be friendly with each other, but it never works out; we just don't *get along*.

to get around

(1) *to go from place to place* *(I/I)*
She certainly *gets around* a lot. Last week she was in Denver; this week she's in Chicago; and next week it'll be Dallas.

(2) *to avoid* *(T/I)*
You'll have to face your problems this time. You can't keep *getting around them* forever.

(3) *to influence or persuade by flattering, etc.* *(T/I)*
Oh, no! You can't *get around me* by saying nice things about me. I'm still not going to let you stay out after midnight.

to get around to

to do something after a delay *(T/I)*
I know that my term paper is due on Monday. I'll *get around to it* over the weekend.

to get at

to find, to discover *(T/I)*
I'm going to *get at the truth,* even if I have to keep investigating the matter for weeks or months.

to get away

to escape *(I/I)*
The robbers had a fast car, so they were able to *get away* from the police.

to get away with

to succeed without being caught or punished *(T/I)*
She tells a lot of lies. I don't know how she *gets away with it,* but everyone always believes her.

to get back at

to get revenge, to even the score with *(T/I)*
I'm trying to think of something I can do to *get back at her* for the terrible things she's said about me.

41

to get by (with)
to *manage, to do something with little work or effort*
(I/I) (T/I)
My job doesn't pay very well, and I'm just *getting by*.
Somehow or other I must learn to *get by with very little
money*.

to get in
(1) *to arrive* (I/I)
The train will *get in* at four-thirty.

(2) *to enter* (I/I)
They lock the door at midnight, so you have to be sure to
get in before then.

(3) *to enter a vehicle* $(I/I$ or $T/I)$
Get in, get in! You can tell me all about it after we *get in
the car*.

to get off
to *dismount* (*from a horse*), *to leave a bus, train, or plane*
$(I/I$ or $T/I)$
If you *get off* at the next stop, you'll be able to walk to
the museum. Those people are going to the museum. You
can *get off the bus* at the same time they do.

to get on
(1) *to mount* (*a horse*), *to enter a bus, train, or plane*
$(I/I$ or $T/I)$
The passengers are *getting on the bus* now. As soon as
they all *get on*, we can leave.

(2) *to grow older* (I/I)
He's really *getting on*. Every time I see him, he looks a
little older than the time before.

to get on with
to *proceed with* (T/I)
You can't just sit there and do nothing. You have to *get
on with your work* if you want to succeed.

to get out (of)

(1) *to leave, to leave a vehicle*   *(I/I) (T/I)*
We'll *get out of class* at four o'clock. After we *get out,* we can play soccer.

(2) *to avoid something unpleasant*   *(T/I)*
Everybody else has to write reports, but she always manages to *get out of it.*

to get over

to recover from   *(T/I)*
I'll feel a lot better after I *get over this cold.*

to get through

to finish   *(I/I or T/I)*
It's taking me a long time to *get through all my work* today. I'll join you just as soon as I *get through.*

to get through to

(1) *to make understand*   *(T/I)*
I've told him over and over again to watch what he's doing, but I can't *get through to him* how important the safety regulations are.

(2) *to reach by telephone*   *(T/I)*
I've dialed her number several times this evening, but I can't *get through to her.*

to get through with

to finish   *(T/I)*
I thought I'd *gotten through with all my work* for the day, and then they brought me another stack.

to get to

(1) *to arrive at*   *(T/I)*
We'll *get to the hotel* early in the evening.

(2) *to make angry*   *(T/I)*
She kept telling me all my faults until it finally *got to me* and I lost my temper.

to get up

(1) *to rise from a sitting or lying position*   *(I/I)*
He always *gets up* from his chair when I enter the room.

(2) *to make rise*   *(T/S)*

I know you have to leave early tomorrow morning. What time do you want me to *get you up?*

to give away

(1) *to make a gift of something*   *(T/S)*

We *give away all the clothes* we don't need any more. We clean out our closets every spring and then *give the old clothes away.*

(2) *to reveal a secret*   *(T/S)*

We wanted to have a surprise party for her, but one of her friends *gave it away,* so it wasn't a surprise to her at all.

to give back

to return   *(T/S)*

I wish you'd *give back the books* you borrowed from me. If you *gave them back,* I could read them myself.

to give in (to)

to yield (to), to stop opposing   *(I/I) (T/I)*

She didn't want to *give in to all the pressure* on her to change her work methods, but when I showed her how much more efficient she could be, she finally did *give in.*

to give off

to emit   *(T/S)*

That machine *gives off some dangerous rays.* We're looking for a way to prevent it from *giving them off* so we can use it safely.

to give out

(1) *to make public*   *(T/S)*

He'll *give out a statement* to the press at noon. After he *gives it out,* he won't have anything more to say on that subject.

(2) *to become used up, finished*   *(I/I)*

The food *gave out* before everybody could be served. We hadn't planned on so many people coming.

(3) *to distribute* *(T/S)*

They're going to *give out the new books* next week. They're waiting until then to *give them out* because they don't have enough copies for everyone yet.

to give up

(1) *to surrender* *(I/I)*

When the police had surrounded him, the thief knew he had to *give up*.

(2) *to part with* *(T/S)*

I don't like to *give up anything* that I've ever owned. If I *give something up*, I feel that I'm losing part of my life.

to give up (on)

to stop trying *(I/I) (T/I)*

I don't like to *give up*, but these problems were so difficult that I had to *give up on them*.

to go about

to get started with, to proceed with *(T/I)*

I don't know how to *go about this job*. I need someone to show me what to do.

to go along (with)

to accompany, to accept someone else's ideas or plans
(I/I) (T/I)

I *went along with the proposal* even though I didn't think it was practical. I *went along* because I knew it would please the boss.

to go around

to be enough for everyone *(I/I)*

The ice cream won't *go around*. There just isn't enough to serve all these people.

to go at

to attack, to work hard at *(T/I)*

I'd like to take a day off, but I have to *go at all this work* that's piled up on my desk.

45

to go back
to return   *(I/I)*
She's the only person I know who likes to *go back* to work
after a vacation.

to go back on
to fail to keep a promise   *(T/I)*
You have to keep your promises. If you *go back on them,*
nobody will trust you.

to go by
(1) *to pass*   *(I/I or T/I)*
The letter carrier just *went by.* He always *goes by our
house* at ten o'clock in the morning.

(2) *to follow*   *(T/I)*
We always *go by the rules* here. We never depart from
them in the slightest degree.

to go for
(1) *to like*   *(T/I)*
She really *goes for him.* She likes him better than anyone
she's ever met.

(2) *to attack*   *(T/I)*
The dog really *went for the letter carrier.* The dog took a
big bite right out of his leg.

to go in for
to engage in, to be interested in   *(T/I)*
She *goes in for sports* in a big way. She's always swimming
or playing tennis or something like that whenever I see
her.

to go into
to investigate, to examine   *(T/I)*
You haven't *gone into this matter* thoroughly enough. You
should look at it again and try to get more information
about it.

to go in with
to share (T/I)
She didn't have enough money to rent an apartment of her own, so she's *going in with two other women*. They'll share a three-bedroom apartment.

to go off
(1) *to explode* (I/I)
The gas exploded without any warning. Several people were hurt when it *went off*.

(2) *to be cut off, to be stopped suddenly* (I/I)
The electricity *went off* during the storm. Luckily we had some candles, so we weren't completely in the dark.

to go on
to happen (I/I)
I wanted to find out what was happening, but there were so many people standing in my way that I couldn't see what was *going on*.

to go on (with)
to continue (I/I) (T/I)
You should *go on with your studies*. If you *go on*, you'll have a good background for the kind of work you want to do.

to go out
(1) *to leave one's house for the purpose of entertainment*
(I/I)
I think she must *go out* every night. She's never at home when I call, and when I do see her, she's at a restaurant or a theater or a party.

(2) *to be extinguished* (I/I)
The lights *went out* without any warning. One second we had lights, and the next we didn't.

(3) *to leave* (I/I)
Be sure and shut the door after yourself when you *go out*.

to go over
to review (T/I)
If you *go over this report* more carefully, you'll get a lot more facts out of it.

47

to go through
   to gain acceptance   *(I/I)*
   His plan *went through* even though there was a lot of opposition to it.

to go through with
   to carry an action to completion   *(T/I)*
   I was going to become a doctor, but I just couldn't *go through with it* because it meant spending too many years in school.

to go under
   to fail, usually a business, etc.   *(I/I)*
   When their sales fell, the company *went under*. It just wasn't making enough money to go on.

to go up
   to increase   *(I/I)*
   Economists disagree about why prices keep on *going up*, and that makes it difficult to work out any policy to prevent prices from increasing even more.

to go with
   (1) *to have a relationship with*   *(T/I)*
   I *went with her* for a long time, but I could never persuade her to marry me, so we finally broke up.

   (2) *to harmonize*   *(T/I)*
   Those two colors don't *go with each other* at all. They look terrible together.

to go without
   to lack, not to have   *(T/I)*
   I had to *go without any amusements* while I was in school because I had just enough money to cover my necessary expenses.

to grow on
   to come to like over a period of time   *(T/I)*
   You may not think much of my plan now, but it will *grow on you*. You'll like it a little bit better every time you think of it.

to grow up
    to become mature   *(I/I)*
    She *grew up* in a small town. She spent all her childhood there, but after she'd finished high school she went to a big city to live and work.

h

to hand down
    (1) *to leave to one's descendants*   *(T/S)*
    His family has *handed down the property* from one generation to another for several hundred years, and he plans to *hand it down* to his oldest son.

    (2) *to give a verdict or judgment*   *(T/S)*
    The judge *handed down the verdict* on Friday morning. He *handed it down* after he had given the case his most careful consideration.

to hand in
    to submit, to give   *(T/S)*
    We have to *hand in our homework* the first thing every morning. Then after we *hand it in,* the teacher tells us the correct answers.

to hand out
    to distribute   *(T/S)*
    I want you to *hand out these instruction sheets.* Go around the room and *hand one out* to each person here.

to hand over
    to yield, to give up   *(T/S)*
    She's *handed over her responsibilities* to another woman. Now that she's *handed them over,* she's ready to retire.

to hang around
    to stay in a place without a purpose   *(I/I or T/I)*
    The young people in the neighborhood *hang around the shopping center* all the time. I don't know why they *hang around* there; there's nothing for them to do.

to hang back

to be slow in coming forward (I/I)

Everybody else wanted to go to the party, but I *hung back* because I wasn't wearing my good clothes.

to hang on

to persevere (I/I)

Most people would have quit when they ran into all those problems, but she *hung on* in spite of all the difficulties.

to hang up

(1) *to place on a hook, hanger, etc.* (T/S)

If you don't *hang up your clothes*, they'll get wrinkled. Here are some hangers that you can *hang them up* on.

(2) *to end a telephone conversation by replacing the receiver* (I/I or T/S)

She didn't want to talk to me, so she *hung up*. And when she did *hang up the phone*, she *hung it up* with a bang to make sure that I got the message.

to happen along/by

to come to a place by chance (I/I)

She always seems to *happen along* just when we're talking about something that we don't want her to hear.

to happen on/upon

to find by chance (T/I)

As we were driving along a country road, we just *happened on this little antique store*, and there's where we found these chairs. It was luck, pure and simple.

to have on

to be wearing (T/I)

They just dropped by. I wasn't expecting them at all, and I *had on* my oldest clothes.

to have over

to invite to one's home, to entertain (T/S)

Shouldn't we ask Marge and Jim to our party? We haven't *had them over* for a long time.

to head off

to prevent or deflect an action　　　　　*(T/S)*

We would like to *head off the auditors* who are going to check our books next week. Perhaps our chairman can *head them off* until we've checked the books ourselves.

to hear from

to get a communication from　　　　　*(T/I)*

I haven't *heard from her* in a long time. I haven't received a call or a letter in weeks.

to hear of/about

to get news or information about, often by chance

(T/I)

Nobody had *heard of their plan* to sell the company until they surprised us with the news at the stockholders' meeting.

to hear out

to hear to the finish　　　　　*(T/S)*

If you'll just *hear me out* instead of interrupting me all the time, you'll find that this is an interesting report.

to help out

to help　　　　　*(I/I or T/S)*

My friends have asked me to *help out* at the neighborhood block party, but if I *help them out*, I'll have to *help out a lot of other people* with their pet projects.

to hit on

to find or discover by chance　　　　　*(T/I)*

That discovery made his reputation, but he just *hit on it*. It wasn't what he expected to find at all.

to hit out (at)

to assail or attack at random　　　　　*(I/I) (T/I)*

He doesn't know who's been making trouble for him. He's just been *hitting out at anyone* that he thinks might be to blame, but he's not making any new friends by *hitting out* all the time.

to hold back

(1) *to restrain, to delay* (I/I or T/S)
You'll have to *hold back* for a while; the sale doesn't begin for fifteen minutes. If you keep on pressing on the doors like this, we'll have to *hold you back* forcibly.

(2) *to keep, to retain, not to reveal* (T/S)
They've been *holding back some important information.* I don't understand why they want to *hold it back* instead of sending it to us.

to hold in

to keep in (one's temper, anxieties, etc.) (T/S)
She never shows what's going on in her mind because she was taught to *hold in her feelings.* But it's not healthy to *hold them in* for too long.

to hold off

(1) *to keep at a distance, to delay* (T/S)
We can't *hold off the directors* much longer. We've been *holding them off* for several months now, but they're beginning to insist on some changes in management.

(2) *to resist an attack* (T/S)
The settlers have *held off the attack* so far. They hope that help will come if they can *hold it off* until sunset.

to hold off (on)

to delay (I/I) (T/I)
I want you to *hold off on your report* for the time being. If you *hold off* for a few days, we'll have more information.

to hold on

(1) *to stop, to wait* (I/I)
Hold on a second! Don't try to go in there until you show us your identification.

(2) *to wait during a telephone conversation* (I/I)
Will you *hold on* for just a moment please. I have a call on another line.

to hold on (to)
to hold   *(I/I)*   *(T/I)*
You've got to *hold on* tight; you can't let go. If you can just *hold on to that branch* for a minute or two more, we'll get help to you.

to hold out
to offer   *(T/I)*
She thinks that her new job *holds out excellent opportunities* for advancement.

to hold out (against)
to keep on resisting   *(I/I)*   *(T/I)*
The employees are *holding out against any changes* in procedures. They'll *hold out* until management stops forcing the changes on them.

to hold out (on)
to keep secret from, to fail to give something
                                           (I/I)   *(T/I)*
Don't *hold out* any more. Tell me what you heard at the meeting. Don't *hold out on me*. I won't tell anyone what you said.

to hold over
(1) *to continue at a later time, to postpone*   *(T/S)*
We decided to *hold over the meeting* until another day because we hadn't had enough time to complete our presentation. If we *hold it over*, we have a better chance of succeeding.

(2) *to keep for a longer time*   *(T/S)*
They're going to *hold over the show* for another week. There's been enough demand for tickets so that they think they can make a little more money by *holding it over*.

to hold up
(1) *to delay*   *(T/S)*
The heavy traffic *held up the bus* to the airport. It *held us up* so long that we missed our flight.

(2) *to hold high*   *(T/S)*
He *held up the sign* above his head. We couldn't see what it said until he *held it up*.

(3) *to rob* (T/S)

Two youths *held up my neighbor* as he was coming home. I think they must be the ones who *held me up* last week.

(4) *to last, to endure* (I/I)

Our procedures have really *held up* over the years. Nobody has felt that it was necessary to make major changes in them.

to hunt down

to pursue until caught (T/S)

They're using dogs to *hunt down the prisoners* who escaped last night. They always manage to *hunt them down* within twenty-four hours.

to hunt out

to search carefully (T/S)

You'll really have to *hunt out all the facts*. It won't be easy to find them, but they're there if you just have the patience to *hunt them out*.

to hunt up

to search for, to look for (T/S)

I *hunted up my cousin* the last time I was in New York. It wasn't easy to *hunt him up* because he didn't have a telephone.

to hush up

to keep secret (T/S)

Everybody has tried to *hush up the scandal*. They think that a lot of people will get hurt if they don't *hush it up*.

i

to invite over

to ask to visit (T/S)

They're usually busy over the weekend, but we can *invite them over* one night during the week.

to iron out

to smooth, to remove difficulties, errors, etc. (T/S)

We still have to *iron out a few discrepancies* in this proposal. We must *iron them out* before we present it to management.

j

to join in
>*to take part in* (I/I or T/I)
>He always *joins in every conversation,* even when he doesn't really know what we're talking about. I've asked him not to *join in* unless he has something to say, but that hasn't stopped him.

to join up
>*to join, usually used of the armed services* (I/I)
>If there's another war, everybody, young or old, man or woman, will have to *join up* for some kind of service.

k

to keep at
>*to continue, to persevere* (T/I)
>She always *keeps at her work* until it's done and done right.

to keep on
>*to continue an action (the action being given in the present participle)* (T/I)
>I *kept on talking* even though I knew that no one was really listening to me any more.

to keep on (with)
>*to continue (with)* (I/I) (T/I)
>They're going to *keep on with their research,* even though the results haven't been satisfactory so far. They feel that if they *keep on,* they'll come up with something valuable.

to keep up
>*to maintain* (T/S)
>It takes a lot of work to *keep up the house,* but if I don't *keep it up,* it will lose some of its value.

to keep up (with)
>(1) *to go at the same speed (as)* (I/I) (T/I)
>You have to try to *keep up with the leader* on these mountain trails. If you don't *keep up,* you may get lost.

He feels it's important to *keep up with everything* that's going on in the world. He *keeps up* by reading every newspaper and magazine he can get his hands on.

(2) *to stay informed (about)*   *(I/I)* *(T/I)*
He feels it's important to *keep up with everything* that's
going on in the world. He *keeps up* by reading every newspaper and magazine he can get his hands on.

to kick around
(1) *to abuse, to treat roughly*   *(T/S)*
After the politician was defeated, he told the press, "Now
you won't be able to *kick me around* any more."

(2) *to discuss*   *(T/S)*
They always *kick a lot of ideas around* at their weekly
meetings.

to kick in
to contribute   *(T/I)*
You have to *kick in your share* of the expenses, or else
you'll have to find another place to live.

to kick off
to begin, to get something started   *(T/S)*
The candidate is going to *kick off his campaign* with a
television speech. He's chosen television to *kick it off* because it will enable him to reach a big audience with just
one appearance.

to kick out
to eject or remove by force   *(T/S)*
They *kicked out the last chairperson* for trying to change
procedures. They'll probably try to *kick you out*, too.

to kick up
to cause trouble or commotion   *(T/I)*
She's not very popular in the office because she *kicks up
a big fuss* whenever anyone else makes a mistake.

to knock out
(1) *to exhaust*   *(T/S)*
All this work has just *knocked me out*. I'm so tired I can't
move.

(2) *to make unconscious* (T/S)

The champion *knocked out his opponent* in the third round of the fight. He *knocked him out* with a hard punch to the jaw.

I

to laugh off

to reject carelessly or thoughtlessly (T/S)

He *laughs off all his troubles.* When things go wrong, he just smiles and jokes about it. Some of his problems are serious, though, so I don't know how he can just *laugh them off.*

to lay away

to put aside or reserve for the future (T/S)

She wants the store to *lay away a coat* for her. She'll make a small downpayment if the store agrees to *lay it away.*

to lay in

to acquire a supply of something for future use (T/S)

I like to *lay in a good supply* of canned food. If I *lay it in,* I feel more secure when the bad weather arrives.

to lay into

to scold (T/I)

She really *laid into me* about the mistakes I made. Nobody's ever given me such a bad time before.

to lay off

to discharge workers (T/S)

Our company *laid off a thousand workers* at the factory last month. We had to *lay them off* because our products have not been selling well.

to lay out

(1) *to spread out* (T/S)

I *laid the pictures out* on the floor so I could see them better.

(2) *to spend* (T/S)

They've *laid out a lot of money* on the campaign. They had to *lay it out* or else their candidate wouldn't have gotten elected.

(3) *to arrange* *(T/S)*

She's working on the organization chart. She's *laying out all the boxes* that show the different positions in the company. After she's *laid them out,* she'll draw lines that show who directs whom and who reports to whom.

to lay over

to stop for a short while on a trip *(I/I)*

It was getting dark, so I began to look for a place to *lay over.* I didn't want to keep on driving after dark.

to lead off

to begin, to come first *(I/I or T/S)*

There are going to be several acts in the show, but they've asked me to *lead off.* If I *lead off the show,* I'll attract a lot of attention. I'll have to give a really striking performance if I *lead it off.*

to lead on

to deceive *(T/S)*

You aren't telling me the truth. You're just *leading me on,* trying to make me believe your story.

to lead up to

to approach something gradually *(T/I)*

I knew that he was *leading up to firing* me, and that he didn't want to hurt my feelings.

to leave off

(1) *to stop doing something* *(T/S)*

We've *left off our research work.* We had to *leave it off* because no more funds were available.

(2) *to deliver or leave something on the way between two places* *(T/S)*

Will you please *leave these letters off* at the post office on your way home.

to leave out

to omit *(T/S)*

You've *left out the most important fact* of all. I don't know how you could have *left it out.* Now you'll have to do the whole report over again.

to lend out
to lend (T/S)
A bank is in business to *lend out money*. When a bank *lends money out*, it makes money by charging interest.

to let down
to disappoint (T/S)
He's *let us down* badly. We thought he'd do a wonderful job, but we're not really pleased with anything he's done.

to let in
to permit to enter (T/S)
It isn't time to open yet, but I think we should *let in the big crowd* in front of the store. If we don't *let them in* now, there may be trouble.

to let off
to allow to escape punishment (T/S)
The jury found him guilty; but the judge *let him off* with a very light sentence.

to let on (to)
to admit to knowing (I/I) (T/I)
I haven't *let on to the surprise* you have for her, and I'm not going to *let on*. Believe me, she'll never find out from me!

to let out
to permit to leave (T/S)
The teacher never *lets out the class* when the bell rings. She only *lets us out* when she's finished with whatever she started to explain.

to let up (on)
to become less, to ease (I/I) (T/I)
The pressure never *lets up*. I have to keep on working all the time, no matter how tired I get. If they don't *let up on me*, I'm going to have a breakdown.

to lie down
to rest in a horizontal position (I/I)
I'm going to *lie down* for a while now. I'm very tired, and I need to rest.

to lie down on
> *to make an insufficient effort* (T/I)
> They think he's been *lying down on the job*. They're sure he isn't doing nearly as much as he could.

to light into
> *to scold vigorously* (T/I)
> The teacher *lit into the students* who hadn't done their homework. She was so angry that she really frightened them.

to light out
> *to leave suddenly* (I/I)
> He just *lit out*. One day he was here and the next he was gone. He didn't even leave an address where we could reach him.

to light up
> *to make light* (T/S)
> Those fireworks really *light up the sky*. They've *lit it up* so much that it looks like daytime.

to line up
> (1) *to get in line* (I/I)
> They told us to *line up* in alphabetical order, but we had a hard time because we didn't all know each other's names.
>
> (2) *to put in line, to put in order* (T/S)
> She has to *line up everything* on her desk when she comes to work in the morning. She can't get any real work done until she *lines everything up*.
>
> (3) *to obtain the services of* (T/S)
> We've *lined up some great performers* for our show. Now that we've *lined them up*, we can begin to advertise the show.

to listen in
> *to listen to another person's conversation on the telephone* (I/I)
> I want you to *listen in* when I talk to the sales manager, but I don't want him to know that you're on the line.

to live down
to overcome a bad reputation (T/S)
He can't *live down his prison record.* Whenever he thinks he's finally *lived it down,* someone starts talking about it again.

to live on
(1) *to maintain life, to support oneself* (T/I)
When they retired they had to *live on a very small income.* They didn't have nearly as much money as they'd been used to.

(2) *to continue to live* (I/I)
When you're young, you expect *to live on and on* forever. It takes a long time to realize that you're really going to grow old.

to live up to
to perform according to a high standard (T/I)
She's coming to us with a wonderful reputation. I hope she can *live up to it.*

to load down
to load too heavily (T/S)
If you *load down the employees* with any more work, some of them may quit. You can't *load them down* and expect them to remain content.

to load up
to load (T/S)
You can *load up the truck* now. After you've *loaded it up,* we'll take all the merchandise to the warehouse.

to look after
to care for (T/I)
I have to *look after the children* this weekend, so I won't be able to go with you. Taking care of them is a full-time job, you know.

to look at
to fix one's visual attention on (*transitive form of* to look)
(T/I)
She was *looking at me* intently; she had her eyes fixed on my face the whole time that I was speaking.

to look back on
to remember (T/I)

I don't *look back on my childhood* with much pleasure. For the most part, I remember it as a time when I was quite unhappy.

to look down on
to feel superior to (T/I)

She *looks down on the other employees* because she had a better education than they did.

to look for
to seek (T/I)

I'm *looking for that report* you want. I don't know what could have happened to it, but it may be in the wrong file.

to look forward to
to anticipate pleasurably (T/I)

They're *looking forward to their vacation.* They're going on a trip that they've been planning and thinking about for a long time, and they're sure they'll have a good time.

to look in (on)
to make a brief visit (to) (I/I) (T/I)

While she was in the hospital I *looked in on her* every evening. I didn't have much time because I was on my way home from work, but at least I *looked in* for a few minutes.

to look into
to investigate (I/I)

Yes, sir, I know you're worried about our declining sales. I'll *look into the matter* immediately. I'll have my department investigate it thoroughly.

to look on
to watch (I/I)

He only *looks on* while other people are doing things. He never participates; he just observes.

to look out
to be careful (I/I)

Look out! Don't cross the street without looking both ways. There's a lot of traffic, so you have to be careful.

to look over

to examine (T/S)

Will you please *look over these letters* for me. After you've *looked them over* and made some notes on them, you can put them in my in-basket.

to look up

(1) *to seek information in a dictionary, etc.* (T/S)

If you don't know how to spell a word, *look it up* in the dictionary. If you are conscientious about *looking up words,* you will soon improve your spelling.

(2) *to find and visit* (T/S)

I have *to look up a lot of old friends* who live in California. I'll *look them up* when I'm out there next month.

to look up to

to respect, to admire (T/I)

I really *look up to her* for everything she's accomplished. She started out with nothing, and she's made a success of everything she's done.

to lose out (on something)/(to someone)

to fail to win (I/I) (T/I)

He's always *losing out.* Last month he *lost out on his chance* for a promotion. To make it worse, he *lost out to the person* he dislikes most in the whole department.

m

to make out

(1) *to discern with difficulty* (T/S)

I can't quite *make out those shapes* over there. Please take a look at them and see if you can *make them out.*

(2) *to write a check, etc.* (T/S)

He *made out the check* for me when I asked for it, but when I took it to the bank, I found that he'd *made it out* wrong.

(3) *to get along, to succeed* (I/I)

No matter what happens, she always *makes out.* When other people are having problems, she just sails right along without any difficulty at all.

to make over

(1) *to make again* (T/S)
I *made over the bookcase* that I spent a whole month on. After I'd finished it, it looked so bad that I decided I had to *make it over.*

(2) *to assign* (T/S)
He *made over some stocks and bonds* to his children. He told me that he wanted to *make them over* while the children were still young so they'd be sure to have enough money for their education.

to make up

(1) *to become friends again after a quarrel* (I/I)
First they fight and then they *make up*. Then, after they've been friendly for a while, they have another fight and then *make up* again.

(2) *to put on cosmetics* (T/S)
I had to *make up my face* with greasepaint when I was in that play. I'd never done it before, so I had to get someone to show me how to *make myself up.*

(3) *to take a course, examination, etc., that one has missed or failed* (T/S)
I was sick on the day of the exam, but the professor wouldn't let me *make it up*. Now I don't know what I'll do. If I can't *make up the exam,* I'll have to take the course over again, and that's a waste of time and money.

(4) *to prepare* (T/S)
Our accountant *makes up the financial statements* every six months. After he's *made them up,* they're sent to all the stockholders.

(5) *to invent, to create* (T/S)
You *made up that story*. Not a word of it is true, I'm sure. You *made it up* from your own head.

to make up for

to compensate for (T/I)
He tries to *make up for his lack of education* by using a lot of big words, but he doesn't always understand what they mean.

to make up to
to try to get the favor of (T/I)
He thinks he can get a promotion by *making up to the boss,* but she's more interested in performance than in flattery.

to map out
to plan (T/S)
I've been trying to *map out a new career* for myself, but every time I think I've *mapped one out,* conditions change so much that my plans are no good any more.

to mark up/down
to raise prices/to lower prices (T/S)
Before the sale they *marked the prices up;* then they *marked them down* for the sale, but the customers were really paying the regular prices.

to measure up (to)
to meet a standard (I/I) (T/I)
You're just going to have to *measure up.* We want the work done according to specifications, and if you can't *measure up to our standards,* we'll have to find someone else to do the work.

to miss out (on)
to fail to be included (I/I) (T/I)
I *missed out on a promotion* again this year. That makes two years that I haven't had a promotion. I wonder how long I'll keep on *missing out.*

to mix up
(1) *to mix, to blend* (T/S)
First you have to *mix up the flour and the eggs.* After you've *mixed them up* thoroughly, you can add the sugar.

(2) *to confuse* (T/S)
She always says so many contradictory things that it *mixes me up* completely. I never know exactly where she stands on the issues.

to mount up
> *to increase* *(I/I)*
>
> Our expenses have been *mounting up* steadily. If we don't cut down on the amount of money we're spending, we won't make a profit.

to move in/to move out
> *to change residence to/to change residence from* *(I/I)*
>
> We wanted to *move in* to our new house tomorrow, but the people who are in it now won't be ready to *move out* for another week.

to move on
> *to leave, to change to a new location, job, etc.* *(I/I)*
>
> When he didn't get a promotion again this year, he decided that the time had come for him to *move on*, so he's already started to look for a new job.

n

to nod off
> *to fall asleep, to doze* *(I/I)*
>
> I was watching television, but I *nodded off*. I just couldn't keep my eyes open.

o

to open up
> (1) *to become open* *(I/I)*
>
> What time will the box office *open up?*

> (2) *to cause to open* *(T/S)*
>
> We have to *open up the store* early tomorrow because of the sale. I've promised to get there in time to *open it up*.

p

to pass away/on
> *to die* *(I/I)*
>
> After the old man *passed away*, his sons and daughters inherited the company and began to make a lot of changes in the way in which it was run.

to pass for
to be mistaken for (T/I)
He speaks so well that he *passes for a person* with a college education, but in fact he never even finished high school.

to pass off
to be accepted (T/S)
She speaks French so well that she can *pass herself off* as a native of Paris.

to pass on
(1) *to make a decision* (T/I)
The court will *pass on that matter* in the near future. You can expect the judge's decision in two or three weeks.

(2) *to convey, to give* (T/S)
She asked me to *pass on this information* to you, but I don't think you should *pass it on* to anyone else. I don't think anyone else needs to know.

to pass out
(1) *to distribute* (T/S)
They're hiring several temporary workers to *pass out these leaflets* to people on the street. They must *pass them all out* before the end of the month.

(2) *to lose consciousness* (I/I)
She was so upset by the news that she *passed out*. It took several minutes for us to bring her to after she'd fainted.

to pass over
to fail to notice, to ignore (T/S)
They *passed over Janet* for a promotion again this year. She knew that there was something wrong because they'd *passed her over* for three years in a row.

to pass up
to fail to take advantage of (T/S)
He's *passed up all the opportunities* they've offered him to do more responsible work. I don't understand why he's *passed them up;* perhaps he feels more secure doing a routine job.

to pay back

to repay (T/S)

I'll *pay back the ten dollars* I owe you on payday. I'm sorry I can't *pay it back* until then.

to pay off

to pay in full (T/S)

She's taken an extra job at night. She needs the money to *pay off her debts*. After she's *paid them off*, she'll quit her second job.

to pay up

to pay (I/I)

He owes me a lot of money. If he doesn't *pay up* pretty soon, I'm going to have to take legal action.

to pick at

(1) *to eat in a fussy way* (T/I)

The children are just *picking at their food*. I don't know why they don't like it well enough to eat properly.

(2) *to nag* (T/I)

My supervisor *picks at me* for every little mistake I make.

to pick on

to find fault with, to tease or criticize (T/I)

People always seem to *pick on anyone* who's different in any way. They criticize the person's behavior or make fun of it until the person begins to act like everyone else.

to pick out

to choose, to select (T/S)

They're meeting to *pick out candidates* to run for election next fall. After they've *picked them out*, the campaign will really get started.

to pick up

(1) *to lift, to raise* (T/S)

He *picked up the chair*, but it was so heavy he couldn't carry it very far. He had to put it down and rest a while before he could *pick it up* again.

(2) *to stop to get someone or something* (T/S)

I'll *pick you up* on my way to the party. Then we won't need to take both our cars.

She *picked up some stamps* while she was at the post office.

(3) *to strike up an acquaintance with* (T/S)

He tried to *pick up the woman* who was waiting for the bus. When he began talking to her, she walked away, and he realized that he wouldn't succeed in *picking her up*.

(4) *to increase, to improve* (I/I)

Our business has really begun to *pick up* since we started advertising more. Our sales have increased about fifty percent.

to pile up

(1) *to accumulate* (I/I)

The work really *piles up* when I'm on vacation. Look at my in-basket — it's full to the top.

(2) *to pile, to place one thing on top of another* (T/S)

Don't *pile up all those boxes!* If you *pile them up* too high, they'll fall down and someone will get hurt.

to pitch in

to set to work with vigor (I/I)

You'll never get your work done if you don't *pitch in*. You can't just sit there and look at it — you have to do some real work on it.

to play down

to make less of something (T/S)

They're *playing down their losses*. They're afraid that if they don't *play them down*, investors will lose confidence in the company.

to play up

to make more of something (T/S)

We should *play up these new safety features* in our advertising. If we *play them up*, people may not notice some of the mechanical problems in our product.

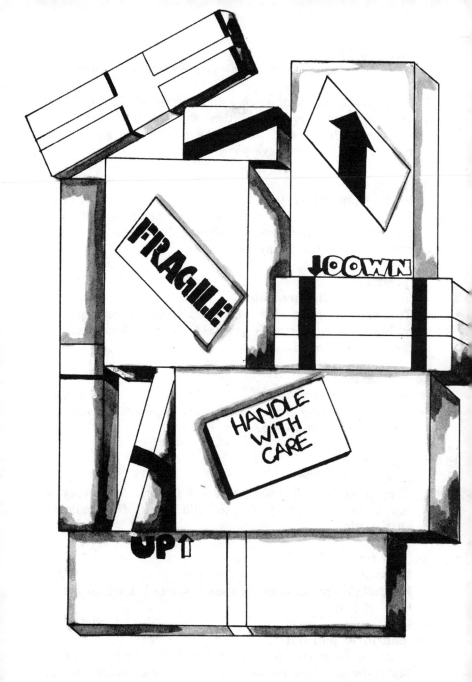

Don't *pile up all those boxes!* If you *pile them up* too high, they'll fall down and someone will get hurt.

to play up to
> to flatter, to try to get someone's favorable attention
> (T/I)
> He certainly has been *playing up to everybody* in the office. He agrees with everything they say and tells them how wonderful they are. I suppose he thinks he'll get a promotion by flattering everyone.

to point out
> to direct attention to (T/S)
> I've *pointed out all the advantages* of my plan, but even though I've *pointed them out* often and vigorously, I'm not sure I've convinced anyone.

to print out
> to print, usually mechanically (T/S)
> This machine *prints out the results* from the computer in multiple copies. After it *prints them out*, we distribute them to the executives.

to pull apart
> to pull into pieces (T/S)
> He was so strong that he *pulled the rope apart* while we were playing tug-of-war.

to pull down
> to demolish (T/S)
> They want to *pull down those old houses*. After they've *pulled them down*, they plan to build a new office building on the site.

to pull for
> to support (T/I)
> I'm *pulling for her*. I'm sure she'll succeed if we all get in back of her.

to pull in/to pull out
> to arrive/to depart (*said of a car, train, etc.*) (I/I)
> My train was just *pulling out* as hers was *pulling in*, so we could only shout a greeting to each other.

to pull off

to bring to a successful conclusion   *(T/S)*

He's trying to *pull off a very dangerous stunt*. If he doesn't *pull it off* just right, he may get hurt.

to pull over

to go to the side   *(I/I)*

The police officer ordered me to *pull over* to the side of the road because I'd been speeding.

to pull through

to survive by a small margin   *(I/I)*

When I had pneumonia, I thought it was the end for me, but I finally *pulled through*. However, it's going to take me a long time before I really feel well again.

to punch in/out

to sign in or out for work on a time clock   *(I/I)*

I didn't get my full week's pay because I *punched in* late on Tuesday and *punched out* early on Thursday.

to push for

to exert pressure in support of something   *(T/I)*

She's always *pushing for her own plans*. She never gives any consideration to any of the ideas that other people propose.

to push on

to advance in spite of difficulties   *(I/I)*

The area was full of swamps and jungle and wild animals, but the explorers *pushed on* nevertheless.

to put across

to convey an idea, etc., so that it can be understood

(T/S)

We want to *put across our arguments* for a budget increase to the board of directors. We think you're the right person to *put them across* in the most convincing way.

to put aside/by

to store or save for future use   *(T/S)*

I *put your letter aside* to answer later, and then I forgot about it.

to put away

to put in the proper place   *(T/S)*
Please *put away your clothes* when you come home. If you *put them away* where they belong, they'll be easy to find when you want them.

to put down

(1) *to lower, to place in a lower position*   *(T/S)*
Put down your umbrella next to the chair. If you *put it down* there, you'll be sure to remember it when you leave.

(2) *to suppress*   *(T/S)*
The government hasn't been able to *put down all the opposition* to its policies. They've tried persuasion, but they may have to use force to *put it down* completely.

to put in

(1) *to spend time in a particular way*   *(T/I)*
He *puts in all the hours* that he's supposed to spend on the job, but he doesn't accomplish very much.

(2) *to install*   *(T/S)*
You can't *put in the dishwasher* by yourself. You've never had any training doing that kind of work. You'll have to call in a plumber to *put it in.*

to put off

to postpone, to delay   *(T/S)*
You shouldn't *put off studying* for your exam. If you *put it off* much longer, the day of the exam will be here, and you won't even have looked at your book.

to put on

to don clothing   *(T/S)*
You should *put on a raincoat* today. If you don't *put one on,* you'll get awfully wet.

to put out

(1) *to extinguish*   *(T/S)*
It took several hours for the fire fighters to *put out the fire.* By the time they'd *put it out,* several of them had been injured.

(2) *to annoy* (T/S)

The delay really *put her out*. She always gets very annoyed when she has to wait for anything.

to put over

to succeed by trickery (T/S)

He thinks he's really *putting something over* on the tax people this time, but he won't be able to fool them when they audit his accounts.

to put through

to get something accepted in spite of opposition (T/S)

They've succeeded in *putting through plans* for the new highway. They *put them through* even though the people in the neighborhood fought against the project.

to put together

to assemble (T/S)

I followed the directions when I tried to *put together the machine*, but when I thought I'd *put it together* correctly, I couldn't get it to work.

to put up

(1) *to build, to erect* (T/S)

They're going to *put up some new houses* on this empty plot of ground. They'll start *putting them up* next year.

(2) *to provide a place to stay* (T/S)

My relatives visit me all the time. I have one room in my house that I can use to *put them up* when they want to stay with me.

to put up with

to endure, to bear, to tolerate (T/I)

I can't *put up with the noise, the traffic, and the pollution* in the city any more. That's why I'm going to move to the country.

to puzzle out

to solve with difficulty (T/S)

I can't *puzzle out these instructions*. I've read them over several times, but they are so complicated that I don't think I'm ever going to be able to *puzzle them out*.

r

to reach out
> to try to achieve an understanding or a relationship
>
> (I/I)

You're going to have to *reach out* if you want to have any new friends. You can't expect people always to come to you; you have to be willing to go to them.

to read out
> to expel from a club, etc. (T/S)

He's been behaving so badly that they're going to *read him out* of the club. They don't want him to come to their meetings anymore.

to read up on
> to obtain facts by reading (T/I)

She's been *reading up on economics*. She thinks it will help her career to know as much as she can learn about economic behavior.

to rent out
> to rent to someone (T/S)

They *rent out their cottage* at the beach one month every summer. When they aren't *renting it out*, they use it themselves.

to ride out
> to survive, to endure (T/S)

We didn't think the prime minister could *ride out the scandal* about his assistants, but he managed to *ride it out* by ignoring the matter completely.

to ring up
> to record a sale on a cash register (T/S)

The clerk will *ring up your merchandise* on the cash register over there. If he doesn't *ring it up* correctly, let me know.

to ring up/down

to raise/to lower the curtain in a theater (T/S)

When we *rang up the curtain,* the audience was very cold to the show, but by the time we *rang it down,* they had become wildly enthusiastic.

to rip into

to scold violently (T/I)

She really *ripped into me* for the things I'd said about her. She left me with no doubt about how angry she was.

to rip up

to tear into pieces (T/S)

I was so angry that I *ripped up your letter* into small pieces so that no one could read it. Now I'm sorry that I *ripped it up.*

to rise up

to rebel (I/I)

The government is afraid the people will *rise up* if the nation's income isn't distributed more equally.

to roll back

to reduce prices, etc., to a previous level (T/S)

The government would like to find a way to *roll back prices* without *rolling wages back,* too.

to roll up

to roll into a ball, etc. (T/S)

I had to *roll up the rugs* before I could clean the floors. My wife helped me *roll them up.*

to rough in/out

to outline in a general or undetailed way (T/S)

We've *roughed out our schedule* for the next year. If you approve of the way we've *roughed the dates in,* we'll go ahead and work out the details.

to round off

to bring to a whole number (T/S)

You should *round off these figures*. You can *round them off* to the nearest dollar. If you have less than fifty cents, just drop the cents; if you have more than fifty cents, use the next highest dollar.

to round out

to complete (T/S)

We want to *round out the membership* in our club. We can *round it out* by taking in three more people; after that there won't be any more vacancies.

to round up

to bring or gather together (T/S)

We tried to *round up the children* but they had scattered all over the park. It took us a long time to *round them up* before we could go home.

to rub in

to emphasize something unpleasant (T/S)

I know I made a mistake, but I wish you'd stop talking about it. You don't need to *rub it in* over and over again.

to rule on

to make a decision in law, etc. (T/I)

The jurors couldn't agree on some of the evidence, so they asked the judge to *rule on some of the points* that were in dispute.

to rule out

to exclude (T/S)

The jury had to *rule out a lot of the evidence* before they could reach a verdict. They *ruled it out* because it was based on hearsay.

to run across/into

to meet or find accidentally (T/I)

I didn't know she was visiting Venice. I just happened to *run across her* in the Piazza San Marco.

to run away (from)

to leave, to escape, to avoid   *(I/I) (T/I)*
She always seems to *run away* whenever I'm around. She leaves before I even get a chance to say a word to her. I hope she isn't *running away from me* because she dislikes me.

to run down

(1) *to seek and find*   *(T/S)*
You need to *run down some more information* to make your thesis acceptable. I think you would be able to *run it down* if you did some more research in the university library.

(2) *to present data, etc., for another person's benefit or information*   *(T/S)*
Just *run down those figures* for me again. I'll understand them better if you *run them down* for me one more time.

(3) *to belittle, to criticize*   *(T/S)*
Don't keep *running her down*. She'll do a better job if you praise her instead of criticizing her all the time.

(4) *to hit with a car, etc.*   *(T/S)*
There's a lot of traffic around here. If you don't keep her on a leash, one of the cars will *run down your dog* sooner or later. They have *run several down* already this year.

(5) *to stop working gradually*   *(I/I)*
That clock is *running down*. You should wind it up if you want it to keep on working.

to run for

to campaign for elective office   *(T/I)*
She's very ambitious. She's going to *run for the state legislature* this year, but she has her eyes on Washington. I wouldn't be surprised if she *ran for president* someday.

to run off

(1) *to make copies on a machine*   *(T/S)*
Please *run off enough copies* of this report for everyone in the office. After you've *run them off*, you can put them on my desk.

We'll have to order more envelopes. We've *run out of them* again. I don't know how we use them up so fast.

(2) *to leave hurriedly* (I/I)

I want to sit down and talk to her, but she's always *running off* in a great hurry.

(3) *to make someone leave hurriedly* (T/S)

When the children tried to play in the old man's yard, he *ran them off*.

(4) *to drain (of water, etc.)* (I/I)

The kitchen sink was stopped up, but the plumber fixed it, so the water's *running off* now.

to run out of

to use the entire supply (T/I)

We'll have to order more envelopes. We've *run out of them* again. I don't know how we use them up so fast.

to run out on

to desert (T/I)

Gauguin wanted to be a painter so much that he *ran out on his family* and left all his responsibilities to them.

to run through

to use or consume rapidly (T/I)

He inherited a lot of money, but he *ran through it* in a couple of years, and now he has almost nothing left.

to run up

to increase rapidly (T/S)

Another wage increase for the workers will *run our costs up* so high that we'll have to raise our prices again.

S

to save up

to save, to accumulate (T/S)

She's *saved up a lot of money*. She's been *saving it up* so that she can take a really luxurious vacation.

to scare away/off

to frighten so as to cause someone to leave (T/S)

The guard *scared off the burglars* who were trying to break into the building. We're very lucky that he managed to *scare them away*.

to scare up

to raise or get with difficulty　　　　　　　　*(T/S)*

He wants to buy a camera, but he can't *scare up the money.*
He's been trying to *scare it up* by borrowing the money
from his friends, but no one will lend him any more.

to screen out

(1) *to eliminate by a process of purification, etc. (T/S)*
We *screen out a lot of impurities* in the water with filters.
If we couldn't *screen them out,* the water wouldn't be
safe to drink.

(2) *to eliminate by a process of examination, etc. (T/S)*
We're *screening out some of the people* who want to get
into the training program. We *screen them out* if they
seem unsuitable after a personal interview.

to see about

to look into, to consider　　　　　　　　*(T/I)*

She's going to *see about my transfer* in a few days, but
she's too busy to consider it right now.

to see off

to watch someone depart　　　　　　　　*(T/S)*

We have to *see off our guests* today. We're going to the
airport to *see them off.*

to see through

to finish, to accomplish a difficult task　　　　　　　　*(T/S)*

Nobody ever thought he'd finish his research project, but
he *saw it through* in spite of all the difficulties that he
encountered.

to see to

to handle, to take care of, to get something done　　*(T/I)*

You don't have to worry about paying the bills. I'll *see to
it.* You can just forget about them.

to sell out

(1) *to sell all of something*　　　　　　　　*(T/S)*

We *sold out all those appliances.* There isn't a single one
left. We *sold them out* because we offered them at bargain
prices.

(2) *to betray a trust for some kind of reward*   *(I/I)*
The candidate we supported in the elections has really *sold out* to the opposition. He never votes the way we expect him to anymore. We don't know why he *sold out* — maybe they offered him money or a position of power.

to send back
to return to the point of origin   *(T/S)*
You'll have to *send back this merchandise;* when merchandise isn't satisfactory, don't hesitate to *send it back.*

to send off
to demonstrate affection, etc., for someone who is departing
(T/S)
When she left the company, they *sent her off* with a big party to show her how much they appreciated all the work she'd done.

to send out
to send, to mail, to distribute   *(T/S)*
They *send out a lot of advertising* every day. They *send most of it out* by mail.

to send over
to send a short distance   *(T/S)*
Yes, we'll *send over the part* that you've been looking for. We'll *send it over* by special messenger.

to send up
to send to prison   *(T/S)*
The judge *sent him up* for five years after the jury had found him guilty.

to set about
to begin a task   *(T/I)*
I'd start assembling this do-it-yourself kit, but I don't know how to *set about it* because I don't understand the instructions.

to set apart
to make different from   *(T/S)*
His experience *sets him apart* from all the other applicants. I'm sure he's the best person for the job.

to set aside

to put to one side for future use (T/S)

I'll *set aside this letter* until I can give it my full attention. I'll *set it aside* with all the other letters I can't get around to.

to set back

to hinder, to check temporarily (T/S)

Her lack of experience *set her back* for a while, but her ability has overcome any disadvantage she may have had to start with.

to set down

to put in writing (T/S)

It's not enough just to tell the workers the procedures they should follow. We have to *set them down* so that everyone can see what they are.

to set forth/off/out

to start a journey, etc. (I/I)

It's getting late. If we don't *set off* in a few minutes, we'll never get home before dark.

to set in

to begin (I/I)

Night *sets in* much more rapidly in the tropics than it does in the temperate zones.

to set off

(1) *to cause to burn or explode* (T/S)

Someone *set off a firecracker* at 3:30 a.m. Whoever *set it off* was trying to scare us.

(2) *to make more apparent by contrast* (T/S)

The white walls really *set the pictures off*, don't they? You can see them much better against a white background.

to set out

to display, to explain (T/S)

After we've *set all the facts out* for you, you'll understand the reasons why we've decided to raise our prices.

to set up
  to establish (T/S)
  We're *setting up a new business,* and we've just been talking to our lawyers because we need legal advice on how we should *set it up.*

to settle down
  (1) *to become calm* (I/I)
  Just *settle down* now. Pacing the floor isn't going to solve your problems. You can think about them a lot better if you're less nervous.

  (2) *to settle in one place* (I/I)
  I don't know where I want to *settle down* when I retire. Sometimes I think about Florida, but it's too hot there in the summer; and sometimes I think about California, but that's too far away from all my friends. I just can't decide where to live.

to settle on/upon
  to reach a decision (T/I)
  There have been a lot of changes in management, but they've finally *settled on new policies* which they intend to stick to for a while.

to settle up
  to pay (I/I)
  It's time to *settle up.* The bills have to be paid before the end of the month, and it's the 28th already.

to settle with
  to reach an agreement, usually about payment; to pay (T/I)
  You have to *settle with us.* If you don't pay what you owe, we're going to have to take you to court.

to shake down
  to extort from (T/S)
  I don't know what he found out about them, but he *shook them down* for a lot of money by promising not to tell what he knew.

to shake off
to get rid of, to ignore (T/S)
He *shook off all the objections* that we made to his new policies. We gave all sorts of reasons for not putting them into effect, but he just *shook them off.*

to shake out
to shake, to remove (T/S)
There are a few problems with your plan. We'll have to *shake them out* before we can put it into effect.

to shake up
to upset (T/S)
His remarks really *shook up the audience.* They *shook me up* so much that I couldn't concentrate on my work all day.

to shape up
to do what is expected of one, to do something properly
(I/I)
You're making too many mistakes. If you can't *shape up* and do your work correctly, we'll have to let you go.

to shave off
to remove by shaving (T/S)
I think you should *shave off your moustache.* You'd look younger if you *shaved it off.*

to ship out
to ship to another location (T/S)
We're *shipping out the merchandise* today. We'll *ship it out* by air so that it will reach you as soon as possible.

to shoot for
to try to achieve a goal (T/I)
We're *shooting for August* to launch our advertising campaign, but we may not be able to get it all together until September or maybe even October.

to shoot off
to shoot (T/S)

No, there isn't a riot going on. They're *shooting the guns off*. They always *shoot them off* when a head of state is visiting.

to show into/out
to escort someone entering or leaving (T/S)

A secretary *showed me into* the office, but there wasn't anyone there to *show me out,* and I had a hard time finding the elevator.

to show off
(1) *to behave in a way that attracts attention* (I/I)

He's always thinking of ways to *show off*. He'd stand on his head if it would make people notice him.

(2) *to display in a way that attracts attention* (T/S)

She likes to *show off her paintings*. She has her house arranged to *show them off* to the best advantage.

to show up
(1) *to arrive unexpectedly* (I/I)

He just *showed up* without any warning. He hadn't sent a letter or a note or anything, and then one evening he was just standing on our doorstep.

(2) *to reveal someone as a fraud or cheat* (T/S)

The newspapers have certainly *shown that politician up* for what he is. They've proved that he never keeps his promises.

to shrug off
to ignore (T/S)

The boss just *shrugged off my suggestions;* she didn't pay any attention to them at all. I'm not going to make any more suggestions if she's going to *shrug them off* like that.

to shut down
to close, usually temporarily (T/S)

They *shut down the factory* last week. They say that they've only *shut it down* for a month or two until business improves, but no one really knows whether it will ever open again or not.

to shut off

to stop the operation of a machine, etc. (T/S)

We have to *shut off the water* now. After we've *shut it off,* we'll get to work on replacing the pipes.

to shut out

to exclude (T/S)

They *shut me out* of their conversation completely. I didn't get a chance to say a word all the time they were talking.

to shut up

(1) *to stop talking* (I/I)

I'm going to *shut up.* I'm not going to say another word. You never listen to me anyway.

(2) *to shut in a confined space, to imprison* (T/S)

I don't let my dogs run around the neighborhood. I *shut them up* in the house until I'm ready to take them for a walk.

to sign away

to dispose of by signing a document (T/S)

He *signed away the rights* to his invention without giving it much thought. He *signed them away* because he never expected his device to make much money.

to sign in/out

to sign a register or log on entering or leaving, or on starting or stopping work (I/I)

I *signed in* when I went into the building at midnight, but I forgot to *sign out* when I left, and nobody stopped me or asked me any questions.

to sign off

to end with a signature or an expression that signals the end (I/I)

The anchorman on the evening news program *signs off* with the same words at the end of every broadcast.

to sign on

to enter into a written agreement to do something

(I/I or T/I)

They've *signed on several members* of the crew for another tour of duty, but I don't think I'm going to *sign on* again because I thought the work was too hard.

to sign over

to assign to someone else by written agreement   *(T/S)*

You'll have to *sign over part of your property* to your ex-wife. If you don't *sign it over*, she'll take you to court.

to sign up

to engage by a written agreement   *(I/I or T/S)*

They're *signing up a lot of people* for their overseas jobs. After they've *signed them up*, they'll get a month's training before they go abroad. I haven't *signed up* yet, though, because I'm not sure I want to work in a foreign country.

to sink in

to become understood slowly   *(I/I)*

You'll have to give me a few minutes for the news of my promotion to *sink in*. It's such good news that I can hardly believe it.

to sit down

to sit, to be seated   *(I/I)*

If I hadn't been *sitting down* when they told me the news, I would have danced all around the room.

to sit in (on)

to be included, usually as an observer   *(I/I) (T/I)*

I was pleased when they told me I could *sit in on the seminar*. I wanted to *sit in* so I could learn more about the subject they were discussing.

to sit out

to remain inactive, not to participate   *(T/S)*

Our organization has decided to *sit out this election*, but if we just *sit it out*, we'll make enemies of those candidates who expected our support.

to sit up

to sit in an upright position, to sit erect   *(I/I)*

Her posture is good because her mother always kept reminding her to *sit up* straight

to size up

to make an estimate   *(T/S)*

The consultants *sized up our problems* after only a few hours. Now that they've *sized them up,* they'll make recommendations to improve our operations.

to sketch out

to sketch, to outline   *(T/S)*

First you have to *sketch out the broad outline* of your proposal. After you've *sketched it out,* you can start to fill in the details.

to skim over

to read or do something superficially   *(T/I)*

You can't just *skim over this report.* You have to read it carefully enough to understand every detail.

to skip out (on)

to run away to avoid a debt, etc.   *(I/I) (T/I)*

He *skipped out on all his obligations.* He left town without telling anyone. Then after he'd *skipped out,* they kept finding he owed money to still more people.

to skip over

to omit   *(T/I)*

Don't *skip over any of this material.* It's important for you to understand all of it.

to slip on/off

to put on or remove clothes quickly   *(T/S)*

It won't take me long to get ready. I just have to *slip this dress off* and then *slip on another.* It'll only take me a minute to *slip it on.*

to slip out

to leave quietly (I/I)

I'm just going to *slip out*. I'll leave without saying anything because I don't want anyone to make a fuss over me when I go.

to slip up (on)

to make an error (I/I) (T/I)

You don't want to *slip up on any of the accounts receivable.* If you *slip up*, it could cost us a lot of money.

to slow down

(1) *to go more slowly* (I/I)

His doctor has told him he has to cut out some of his activities. If he doesn't *slow down*, he could have a heart attack.

(2) *to make go more slowly* (T/S)

They've *slowed down their rate of production*. They had to *slow it down* because they had too large an inventory.

to slow up

(1) *to go more slowly* (I/I)

I told him to *slow up* because he was driving much too fast.

(2) *to make go more slowly* (T/S)

The police are trying to *slow up traffic* on the highways. If they succeed in *slowing it up*, there will be fewer accidents.

to smash up

to smash or wreck completely (T/S)

He really *smashed up his car*. It's a total wreck. It's too bad he had to *smash it up* just before leaving on a long trip.

to smoke out

to discover in order to bring to public knowledge (T/S)

The reporters are trying to *smoke out the truth* of the politician's financial dealings. If they can *smoke it out*, there's probably going to be a big scandal.

91

to smooth over
> *to make something bad or unpleasant appear less serious*
> (T/S)
> She's very good at *smoothing over disputes* among her friends. She says a word here and there and we suddenly find that she's *smoothed everything over* so that no one's angry anymore.

to snap out of
> *to recover quickly* (T/I)
> You have to *snap out of this bad mood* of yours. If you don't *snap out of it* pretty soon, you won't have any friends left.

to snap up
> *to seize eagerly* (T/S)
> The customers *snapped up all the merchandise* we had on sale. They *snapped it up* so fast that we were sold out by noon.

to sneak up (on)
> *to approach quietly or stealthily* (I/I) (T/I)
> Don't *sneak up* like that. Every time you *sneak up on me*, it startles me so much that I drop something.

to soak up
> *to absorb* (T/S)
> Let me have a paper towel so I can *soak up this coffee* I spilled. If I *soak it up* quickly it won't leave a stain.

to sort out
> *to sort, to arrange by classification* (T/S)
> Please *sort out these bills* according to date. After you've *sorted them out*, you can put them on my desk.

to sound off
> *to state loudly, emphatically* (I/I)
> You can hear him talking at every meeting we have. He *sounds off* about everything, whether he knows anything about it or not.

Let me have a paper towel so I can *soak up this coffee* I spilled. If I *soak it up quickly*, it won't leave a stain.

to sound out

to attempt cautiously to discover someone's feelings or opinions (T/S)

We should try to *sound out all the members* about the changes in the rules. We don't want to take a vote until after we've *sounded them out*.

to space out

to extend by using more space or time (T/S)

You should learn to *space out your activities* through the whole day instead of doing everything in the morning. You always get tired at noon because you haven't *spaced things out* enough.

to speak for

to speak on behalf of, to represent (T/I)

She won't admit it, but I'm sure she's *speaking for a high government official* who doesn't want to be quoted directly.

to speak out

to make one's opinions known (I/I)

You should *speak out* and let management know what you think about that project. If you don't let people know what you think, it'll be too late to make any changes.

to speak up

to speak louder (I/I)

They told the lecturer to *speak up* because they couldn't hear her in the back of the room.

to speed up

(1) *to go faster* (I/I)

Don't try to *speed up* until we've gone around this curve — it's a dangerous one.

(2) *to make go faster* (T/S)

The efficiency experts are trying to *speed up the rate of production*. They say they can *speed it up* if management provides more incentives for the workers.

to spell out
to explain in detail *(T/S)*
You must *spell out your proposal* if you want to get it accepted.

to spice up
to make more interesting or shocking *(T/S)*
The reporter *spiced up his account* of the accident with a lot of gory details. The accident was so terrible, though, that he didn't really need to *spice it up*.

to spin out
to make longer, to extend *(T/S)*
She likes to *spin out a story* by including every little detail she can think of, but the more she *spins it out*, the more boring it becomes.

to split off
to separate *(T/S)*
They *split off our section* of the company and set it up as a separate corporation. They found there was a tax advantage in *splitting it off*.

to split up
(1) *to split or divide into pieces* *(T/S)*
We should *split up that difficult job* among several employees. If we *split it up*, it's sure to get done faster.

(2) *to separate (used of people)* *(I/I)*
They're going to *split up*. They can't get along together anymore, so they're going to separate.

to spread out
to extend over a large area or time *(T/S)*
She wanted to *spread out the drawings* so that everyone could see them. She finally decided to *spread them out* on the floor.

to spring up
(1) *to leap or jump up* *(I/I)*
He *springs up* whenever one of his superiors comes into the room. He thinks he can impress them by showing how polite he is.

(2) *to grow suddenly, rapidly* (I/I)

Those children have certainly *sprung up* since I saw them last year! Why, they were only babies then!

(3) *to come into existence suddenly or rapidly* (I/I)

New housing developments seem to *spring up* overnight on the edges of the suburbs. One day you see open fields, and the next day the builders are at work.

to spruce up

to improve the appearance of (T/S)

It's going to cost me some money to *spruce up my house,* but I can get a better price if I *spruce it up* before I put it up for sale.

to square off

to get into a position to fight (I/I)

Those two are always *squaring off.* You think they're going to start fighting the next instant, and instead they burst into laughter.

to square up

to adjust or settle debts, etc. (T/S)

You should *square up your accounts.* You'll feel a lot better when you pay off your debts and *square everything up.*

to stack up

(1) *to pile one thing on top of another* (T/S)

Just *stack up the dishes.* I'll put them in the dishwasher later, but it will help if you *stack them up* now so they won't take up so much space.

(2) *to come to a correct conclusion* (I/I)

These facts just don't *stack up.* Either your conclusion is wrong or the facts are inaccurate.

to stake out

(1) *to claim as one's territory* (T/S)

She's *staked out that corner* of the office for herself. She *staked it out* by moving all her files and equipment into it.

(2) *to put under surveillance* (T/S)

The police have *staked out the bank* all week. They have officers watching it from several different places. They decided to *stake it out* because they got a tip that someone was going to try to rob it.

to stall off

to evade or put off (T/S)

They're asking for an answer today. You can't *stall them off* any longer. You'll have to tell them what they want to know today.

to stamp out

(1) *to make something by pressing with a heavy weight* (T/S)

The panels for the car doors are made by *stamping them out* on a huge metal press.

(2) *to crush* (T/S)

During the course of history, authority has used many methods to *stamp out opposition,* but they never have and never will *stamp it out* completely as long as human beings keep on thinking.

to stand by

(1) *to wait for an emergency* (I/I)

A good part of a fire fighter's day involves just *standing by* and being ready in case someone turns on a fire alarm.

(2) *to wait for a flight on an airline* (I/I)

We had to *stand by* for the flight. We had to wait until all the passengers with confirmed reservations had boarded to see if there were any seats for us.

to stand for

(1) *to represent* (T/I)

The abbreviation "e.g." *stands for the Latin expression exempli gratia,* which means "for example."

(2) *to bear, to endure* (T/I)

They won't *stand for much more of your sloppiness.* If you can't learn to do your work correctly, they'll fire you.

97

to stand in (for)

to fill someone else's position or duty   *(I/I) (T/I)*

I'm just *standing in*. Our senior official couldn't attend the meeting, so I'm *standing in for her*. That's why I'm not too well informed about the problems you're discussing.

to stand off

to resist until a tie or draw has been reached   *(T/S)*

Our defense was able to *stand off their offense*. They *stood them off* through the whole game, and it finally ended in a tie.

to stand out

(1) *to be especially noticeable*   *(I/I)*

With that red dress on, you'll really *stand out* in the crowd. I won't have any trouble locating you.

(2) *to be noticeable because of superior quality*   *(I/I)*

Her work always *stands out*. It's always top-notch. It's better than the work of anyone else in the class.

(3) *to continue to oppose*   *(I/I)*

The jury couldn't reach a verdict because one of the jurors was *standing out*. That juror didn't believe that the defendant was guilty.

to stand up

(1) *to rise to a standing position*   *(I/I)*

You should *stand up* when the president comes into the room. Don't stay in your seat.

(2) *to stand erect*   *(I/I)*

Stand up! Don't slouch like that! Your posture is terrible.

(3) *to last, to bear up, to endure*   *(I/I)*

The plastic in my kitchen has really *stood up*. I had it put in five years ago, and it doesn't show any signs of wear yet.

(4) *to fail to keep an engagement*   *(T/S)*

I was supposed to meet her at five o'clock, but she *stood me up*. She didn't show up or call or anything.

to stand up for

to defend, to support (T/I)

I expect you to *stand up for me* at the meeting. If they attack me for the way I've been doing my job, I want you to say some good things about my performance.

to stand up to

to resist, to encounter successfully (T/I)

She's really *standing up to all the pressures* of her job. We thought she might not be able to handle all the deadlines, but she's met every one of them without getting even slightly upset.

to start out

to leave on a voyage, etc. (I/I)

What time do you want to *start out?* Do you want to leave early or late?

to start out on

to begin a voyage, a career, etc. (T/I)

He's acquired a tremendous amount of experience because he was very young when he *started out on his career.*

to start up

to get something started (T/S)

He enjoyed *starting up the business,* but he lost interest in it after he'd *started it up* and it was running smoothly.

to stay over

to remain in a place for an additional period of time

(I/I)

They were enjoying their trip to Puerto Rico so much that they *stayed over* two extra days.

to stay up

to remain without going to bed (I/I)

How can you *stay up* so late every night? If I *stayed up* every night until one or two o'clock the way you do, I'd never get to work on time.

to steal up (on)

to approach silently, stealthily (I/I) (T/I)

Make some kind of noise when you come into the room. Don't *steal up* that way. It really startles me when you *steal up on me* without any warning.

to step aside

(1) *to move to one side* (I/I)

If you *step aside*, I'll be able to see better.

(2) *to allow someone else to get credit, etc.* (I/I)

He's not at all selfish. When it came time to get credit for the invention, he *stepped aside* and let the others get the glory.

to step down

to retire (I/I)

He's been head of the company for a long time, but he's going to *step down* next year, and no one knows who'll take his place.

to step in

to visit for a brief time (I/I)

I'll just *step in* to see how you are. I won't stay more than a minute.

to step into

to have unexpected good fortune (T/I)

She just *stepped into that job*. She didn't really know what her duties were going to be, but it turned out to be exactly right for her. It uses all her talents, and she's doing the work brilliantly.

to step on

to suppress (T/I)

We're going to *step on any opposition* before it gets a chance to start. We won't put up with any contrary opinions even for a moment.

to step up

to increase (T/S)

The newspapers have *stepped up their attacks* on our candidate. I suppose they've *stepped them up* because he seems to be winning some popular support.

to stick around

to remain in the same place   *(I/I)*

Stick around a little longer. I'll be finished in about five minutes, and then I can go with you.

to stick by

to remain true or faithful   *(T/I)*

She *stuck by me* through all my troubles. She never doubted that things would turn out right for me in the end.

to stick out

to be noticeable, often in a bad way   *(I/I)*

That new building really *sticks out* in this neighborhood. It doesn't fit in at all with all these nice old houses.

to stick to

to persist, to persevere   *(T/I)*

It takes a long time to learn a language. You have to *stick to it.* You don't really learn much if you get discouraged and quit after a year or so.

to stick up

to rob, to hold up   *(T/S)*

A couple of thugs tried to *stick me up* last night, but when I shouted for help, they ran away.

to stick up for

to defend, to support   *(T/I)*

None of the others *stuck up for our proposal,* so it was voted down by a big margin.

to stir up

to arouse, to incite   *(T/S)*

He's a wonderful speaker. He can *stir up people's emotions* with only a few words. The government doesn't like it, though, when he does *stir the people up.*

to stock up (on)

to lay in a supply (*of*)   *(I/I) (T/I)*

We need to *stock up on food* for the winter. If we *stock up* now, we'll have enough to eat if we get snowed in.

to stop off

to make a short stop during a journey *(I/I)*
While we were on our way to the beach, we *stopped off* at our friends' house just long enough to say hello.

to stop over

to make a stop on a journey with the privilege of using the same ticket to continue *(I/I)*
We were making a trip from Chicago to San Francisco, but when we found we could visit Denver without paying anything extra, we decided to *stop over* there to see some friends.

to stop up

to cause to become clogged *(T/S)*
All that paper *stopped up the drain*. I told him it would *stop it up*, but he threw it into the sink anyway.

to store up

to store *(T/S)*
Squirrels *store up a lot of nuts* in the fall. They *store them up* so they'll have a supply of food all winter long.

to stow away

(1) *to put away, to put in the proper place* *(T/S)*
After he brings his boat into port, he *stows away all the gear* so that everything is shipshape. He usually *stows it away* in those big chests.

(2) *to conceal oneself on a ship or airplane in order to secure free passage* *(I/I)*
After the ship had left port, they found two people who had *stowed away* in one of the lifeboats. They wanted to get to the island, but they didn't have enough money to pay their way.

to straighten out

(1) *to correct, to put in order* *(T/S)*
You can *straighten out your ideas* later. For now just put things down in any order. We'll get someone to help you *straighten things out* when you're ready to prepare the final version of the report.

(2) *to become orderly, reliable, etc.* *(I/I)*
I don't know what's going to happen to that young man if
he doesn't *straighten out*. Right now his life is in a terrible
mess.

(3) *to cause to become orderly, reliable, etc.* *(T/S)*
Do you think you can help to *straighten out that young
man*? He certainly can't *straighten himself out*. He just
goes from one problem to another.

to straighten up
to make straight, neat, correct *(T/S)*
She never *straightens up the kitchen* after she prepares
a meal. She just leaves the mess until someone else comes
along to *straighten it up* for her.

to stray away/off
to wander *(I/I)*
That child is always *straying away*. Her parents never
know where she's going to get to, but they still don't keep
an eye on her.

to stretch out
(1) *to extend one's body to full length* *(I/I)*
Oh, but it feels good just to lie here on the grass and
stretch out! I can feel every muscle in my body relax.

(2) *to extend* *(T/S)*
I *stretched out the cloth* to see if I had enough to make a
slipcover for the couch. When I *stretched it out,* I noticed
several imperfections. I guess I'll have to return it to the
store.

to strike out
to eliminate with the stroke of a pen, etc. *(T/S)*
You should *strike out this paragraph*. Your report will be
a great deal more forceful if you *strike it out*.

to strike out (at)
to attack indiscriminately *(I/I) (T/I)*
When she's angry, she *strikes out at anyone* who comes
near her, whether or not the person was responsible for
making her lose her temper. She's got to learn, though,
not to *strike out* like that.

to strike up

to cause to begin (T/I)

When you travel, you often *strike up friendships* with the people you meet, but they're usually not the kind of friendships that last very long.

to string out

to extend for too long a time (T/S)

The professor *strung out the lecture* so long that I nearly fell asleep before he finished. I don't know why he *strings things out* like that.

to string up

to hang, to kill by hanging (T/S)

The mob *strung up the outlaws* without giving them any sort of trial. After *stringing them up*, they celebrated in the nearest saloon.

to strip off

(1) *to strip, to remove by stripping* (T/S)

We must *strip off the old paint* on this desk. If we don't *strip it off*, refinishing it will be a waste of time.

(2) *to remove one's clothing* (T/S)

My clothes got wet through in the storm. When I came in, I *stripped them off* in a hurry so I wouldn't catch a chill.

to stumble across/on/upon

to find or encounter accidentally (T/I)

He was doing a completely different experiment when he *stumbled on the discovery* that made him famous.

to sum up

to make a brief, final presentation of the facts

(I/I or T/S)

The professor is finally beginning to *sum up*. He said he was going to *sum up his arguments* half-an-hour ago, but he's still talking. I don't think he knows how to *sum things up* in a few brief sentences.

to summon up
to arouse (T/S)
The candidate can't *summon up any enthusiasm* among the voters. Unless he's able to *summon some up* before the election, he's going to lose by a wide margin.

to swear in
to put someone in office by administering an oath (T/S)
He's already begun to carry out his official duties. The president *swore him in* yesterday morning.

to swear off
to make a pledge to abstain from something (I/I or T/I)
He's *sworn off smoking*. He knew that it would be bad for his health if he didn't *swear off*.

to sweep out
to clean the inside of something by sweeping (T/S)
You didn't *sweep out the office* last night. I told you I wanted you to *sweep it out* every night.

to sweep up
to sweep (T/S)
We have to *sweep up this trash* now. We won't be able to do any more work in here until we *sweep it up*.

to switch on/off
to connect or disconnect an electric device by means of a switch (T/S)
Don't *switch on the lights* until you've *switched off the air conditioner*. You'll blow a fuse if you don't *switch it off* first.

t

to tag along
to follow, to accompany, often when not wanted (I/I)
There aren't any children his own age in the neighborhood, so he *tags along* with an older group, even though he can't always keep up with them.

to take after

to resemble, to have the traits of   (T/I)

That little girl really *takes after her grandmother.* She not only looks like her, she acts like her too.

to take away

to remove   (T/S)

You can *take away the dishes* now. After you've *taken them away,* please bring the dessert.

to take back

(1) *to return*   (T/S)

I have to *take back these slacks.* They don't fit me, and I've decided to *take them back.*

(2) *to withdraw or retract something said*   (T/S)

I told him to *take back what he said* or I'd beat him up. He *took it back.*

to take down

(1) *to remove from a high place*   (T/S)

Will you help me *take down my suitcase?* It's on the top shelf of my closet, and I have to *take it down* before I can start packing.

(2) *to put in writing*   (T/S)

You have to be careful what you say in the meeting. A secretary will be there to *take down everything* that is said. She'll *take it down* so that there'll be a record of who said what.

to take in

(1) *to understand*   (T/S)

I didn't *take in all the points* the lecturer was making. I tried to follow what she was saying, but she was speaking so fast that I couldn't *take it all in.*

(2) *to deceive*   (T/S)

No matter what stories you tell him, you can *take him in.* He believes just about everything he hears.

You have to be careful what you say in the meeting. A secretary will be there to *take down everything* that is said. She'll *take it down* so that there'll be a record of who said what.

(3) *to receive, to find a place for* (T/S)

The mission will *take in anyone who needs help*. They feel that it is their duty to *take them in* and feed them, find a place for them to stay, and help them to get straightened out.

to take off

(1) *to leave* (I/I)

She keeps looking at her watch because she wants to *take off* at exactly five o'clock.

(2) *to leave the ground (an airplane)* (I/I)

After the plane *takes off*, it'll be about fifteen minutes before it reaches its cruising altitude; then they'll serve drinks.

(3) *to get off to a good start, to increase suddenly* (I/I)

After they started to advertise on television, their sales really *took off*.

(4) *to remove one's clothing* (T/S)

You should *take off your hat* in the elevator. If you don't *take it off*, people will think you're impolite.

(5) *to take time from work, school, etc.* (T/S)

I have to *take a day off* from work next week. I can't get all the work around the house done if I go in to work every day.

to take on

(1) *to hire* (T/S)

The company is *taking on additional employees*. They're *taking them on* because sales have increased dramatically.

(2) *to agree to do or handle* (T/S)

She's always *taking on more work* than she can handle. I don't know why she keeps *taking it on* when she can't finish up what she's already doing.

to take out

(1) *to remove* (T/S)

You should *take out the meat* in about two hours. If you forget to *take it out*, it will lose all of its flavor.

(2) *to escort for social purposes* *(T/S)*
He's *taken out his secretary* three nights this week. He must really like her, or he wouldn't *take her out* so much.

to take over

to assume control of *(I/I or T/S)*
A new management is going to *take over the company*, and we expect a lot of changes when they *take it over*. We don't know when they'll *take over*, but it should be soon.

to take to

(1) *to feel friendly to* *(T/I)*
The first time I met her, I *took to her*. I liked her right from the beginning.

(2) *to get into the habit of, to become addicted to* *(T/I)*
Since I *took to going to bed* early, I have a hard time staying awake after eleven o'clock at night.

to take up

(1) *to start an activity* *(T/S)*
She *took up pottery* last year. She's made some beautiful things since she *took it up* seriously.

(2) *to start discussing* *(T/S)*
We want to *take up that matter* at our next meeting. You can say all you want about it when we *take it up* then, but let's not discuss it now.

to talk back (to)

to answer in a rude manner *(I/I) (T/I)*
Those children are always *talking back to their parents*. I never heard anything so rude! They should teach them some manners so they won't *talk back* all the time.

to talk down to

to talk to someone in a childish or condescending manner
(T/I)
You don't need to *talk down to me*. I'm intelligent enough to understand your ideas without having them simplified.

to talk out
to resolve by talking (T/S)
She has a lot of problems, but she's trying to *talk them out* with her psychoanalyst.

to talk up
(1) *to talk louder* (I/I)
Talk up! I can't hear a word you're saying.

(2) *to promote by talking* (T/S)
She's always *talking up her own schemes* to make people adopt them. She *talks them up* to everyone in the office, but she never pays any attention to what people really think of her ideas.

to team up
to form into a team (I/I)
They asked me to *team up* with Nadia and Oscar so we could work together on the research project, but I'm not sure I could collaborate successfully with either of them.

to tear down
to demolish (T/S)
We have to move because they're going to *tear down the building*. They're going to begin to *tear it down* in November.

to tear into
to attack angrily (T/I)
The other people at the meeting really *tore into me* when I said I didn't like their plans. I don't know why they were so angry.

to tear up
to tear or rip into small pieces (T/S)
She *tore up the letter* as soon as she read it. She *tore it up* because it made her angry.

to tell off
to scold severely (T/S)
She lost her temper with me again and said some things I won't forget. If she *tells me off* again, I'm going to quit.

to tell on

to report someone else's misdeeds (T/I)

We were both playing in the street, so you can't *tell on me* or you'll get into trouble, too.

to thaw out

(1) *to melt* (I/I)

There's a lot of ice on the sidewalk, but it's beginning to *thaw out*.

(2) *to become less cold or reserved* (I/I)

When I first met her, she hardly spoke to me, but I think she's beginning to *thaw out* now. She seems a lot more cordial than she did.

(3) *to cause to melt* (T/S)

It'll take all day to *thaw out this steak*, but you can't cook it while it's still frozen. You have to *thaw it out* first.

to thin down

to make thin (T/S)

I've gone on a diet so I can *thin myself down*.

to thin out

to make thin, less crowded (T/S)

You should *thin out these flowers*. You've got too many in this pot, and if you don't *thin them out*, they'll never bloom.

to think out

to think to a conclusion (T/S)

You haven't *thought out this plan* for the house carefully enough. If you'd *thought it out* better, you would have provided more closet space.

to think over

to give continued thought to something in order to reach a decision (T/S)

I hear you're *thinking over the idea* of quitting. I hope you *think it over* very carefully. You shouldn't decide anything hastily.

to think through
to think to a conclusion or a solution (T/S)
You'll see the answer if you just *think the problem through*.

to think up
to devise (T/S)
She *thought up a really great advertising slogan* for the company. She said she *thought it up* while she was driving to work this morning, but it's probably been at the back of her mind for a long time.

to throw away
to discard (T/S)
Don't *throw away those newspapers*. I haven't had time to look at them yet. I'll *throw them away* when I've finished reading them.

to throw off
to recover from (T/S)
I'm trying to *throw off a cold*. I'm sure I can *throw it off* by taking a lot of Vitamin C.

to throw out
(1) to discard (T/S)
What are you doing? Don't *throw out all those books*. There may be something there I want to read. Let me look them over before you *throw any more out*.

(2) to eject forcibly (T/S)
When he started to shout at the waiter, the manager told him they'd *throw him out* if he didn't behave himself.

to throw over
to break a relationship suddenly or abruptly (T/S)
Everybody thought they were going to get married, but then she *threw him over* for someone we'd never met.

to throw up
to vomit (I/I)
The baby's been *throwing up*. I think we should call the doctor right away.

to tide over
to get someone through a difficult period (T/S)
It would help if you could lend me twenty dollars. That would be enough to *tide me over* until payday.

to tie down
(1) *to make definite* (T/S)
The sales representative is sure she's going to make a big sale, but she hasn't *tied it down* yet. She still hasn't got the purchaser to sign a sales order.

(2) *to restrict one's freedom of action* (T/S)
He never keeps his friends very long because he says that he doesn't want to have any relationship that will *tie him down.* He says he likes to be free to do what he wants without thinking about anyone else.

to tie up
(1) *to tie, to bind with ropes, etc.* (T/S)
The burglars who broke into the house *tied me up* with my own neckties.

(2) *to prevent from doing something else* (T/S)
That meeting will *tie me up* all morning. I won't be able to get anything else done until it's over.

(3) *to stop* (T/S)
I'm late because there was an accident on the freeway that *tied traffic up* for more than an hour.

to tighten up
to make tighter (T/S)
You should *tighten up these screws.* If you don't *tighten them up,* your wheel may come off.

to tip off
to warn, to give secret information about (T/S)
The robber didn't know who *tipped off the police,* but he knew someone had *tipped them off* when he found himself surrounded.

to tip over
to cause to fall or tilt to one side (I/I or T/S)
Everybody began to run when they saw that the tree was *tipping over.* The wind from the storm *tipped it over.*

All the hard work in this terrible heat really *tired me out.*

to tire out
   to exhaust (T/S)
   All the hard work in this terrible heat really *tired me out*.

to tone down
   to make less strong or intense (T/S)
   Some of the things you've written will really make people angry. You should *tone down your report* to make it more acceptable, but I realize that *toning it down* won't be easy for you.

to tone up
   to make stronger or healthier (T/S)
   These exercises have really *toned me up*. I feel better than I've felt in a long time.

to toss off
   to make suggestions, etc., casually or at random (T/S)
   She's always *tossing off good suggestions*. I don't know how she thinks of them, but she can *toss an idea off* whenever anybody needs one.

to toss up
   to throw a coin in the air to make a decision (T/S)
   Do you have a quarter? Go ahead and *toss it up*. If it comes down heads, we'll do it my way, and if it comes down tails, we'll do it yours.

to touch off
   to start something bad (T/S)
   The government doesn't know who *touched off the riot*. Some people think the police *touched it off*, but others say that the demonstrators really started it.

to touch on/upon
   to mention briefly (T/I)
   I went to the lecture so I could learn something about the copyright law, but the speaker just *touched on the subject* and went on to other things after a sentence or two.

to touch up

to improve in small ways (T/S)

That table isn't in such bad shape. You only need to *touch it up* here and there with a little paint to make it look really good.

to track down

to hunt, to pursue by following a trail or tracks (T/S)

They're going to use dogs to *track down the criminals.* The dogs *track them down* by following their scent.

to trade in

to use something old as partial payment for something new (T/S)

I really need a new typewriter. I think I'll *trade in my old one* for a new one. If I didn't *trade it in,* I wouldn't be able to afford a new one.

to trade on/upon

to use one's reputation, etc., to advantage (T/I)

He's still *trading on the work* he did twenty years ago. He hasn't done anything new, but he can still get jobs on the basis of that old stuff.

to trip up

to catch in a lie (T/S)

I told her I didn't come to work yesterday because I was sick, but she *tripped me up* because she'd seen me going to the movie.

to try on

to test the fit or appearance of (T/S)

You should *try the coat on* before you buy it. Unless you *try it on,* you won't know if it fits properly.

to try out

to test, to experiment with (T/S)

They've *tried out several people* in that job, and none of them has done very well, but I think you can do it, so I'm going to recommend that they *try you out.*

to tune in/out
to adjust the controls of a radio, etc.   *(T/S)*

I've just *tuned in this program,* and I want to listen to it. If you play with the dial, you'll *tune it out.*

to tune up
(1) *to adjust the sound of a musical instrument*

                                (I/I or T/S)

The orchestra is *tuning up.* The musicians have to *tune up their instruments* before the concert, but it will only take a few minutes to *tune them up.*

(2) *to adjust an engine, etc.*   *(T/S)*

I'm going to take my car to the garage today so the mechanic can *tune it up* before I leave on my trip.

to turn down
(1) *to reject, to refuse*   *(T/S)*

I've been trying to get into the management training program, but the personnel department keeps *turning me down*; I don't know whether I'll ever get the chance to go into the program.

(2) *to make less loud, less strong, etc.*   *(T/S)*

Pleased *turn down the radio.* If you don't *turn it down,* I won't be able to do my work.

to turn in
(1) *to go to bed*   *(I/I)*

It's getting late, and I'm getting sleepy. I'm going to *turn in* now. I'll see you in the morning.

(2) *to submit*   *(T/S)*

We *turn in our homework* at the beginning of class. After we've *turned it in,* the teacher reviews yesterday's lesson.

(3) *to report or hand over to authority*   *(T/S)*

He didn't believe his friends would ever betray him, but one of them *turned him in* to the police.

to turn into
to become   *(T/I)*

It was cloudy this morning, but it's really *turned into a nice day.*

to turn off

to stop the flow of, to extinguish a light (T/S)
Why didn't you *turn off the water?* I found the bathtub overflowing and I had to *turn it off* for you.

to turn on

to start the flow, to put on a light (T/S)
Don't *turn on the lights* until it gets darker. You'll just waste electricity if you *turn them on* now.

turn on/upon

to attack without warning (T/I)
I thought I was getting along with him really well. Then one day he just *turned on me.* He said some terrible things, and now I don't want to see him any more.

to turn out

(1) *to extinguish a light* (T/S)
I haven't *turned out the lights* yet. I'll *turn them out* before I turn in.

(2) *to produce* (T/S)
It takes several workers to *turn out the radios.* They're considering cutting the work force by using automated equipment to *turn them out.*

(3) *to eject, to evict* (T/S)
They *turned out several families* from this apartment building last month. They *turned them out* because they hadn't paid their rent.

(4) *to remove from public office, etc.* (T/S)
The voters don't think much of their representative. They'll probably *turn him out* at the next election.

(5) *to result* (I/I)
I don't know how this experiment is going to *turn out,* but I'll keep on working at it until I get some sort of result.

(6) *to attend, to appear* (I/I)
So many people *turned out* for the rock concert that the police sent extra officers to control the crowd.

to turn up

    (1) *to discover by chance*   *(T/S)*

    They've *turned up some interesting artifacts*. They *turned them up* when they were excavating for a new building. Nobody had expected to find anything there.

    (2) *to be in a place unexpectedly, to arrive unexpectedly*   *(I/I)*

    I keep seeing her all the time. She seems to *turn up* wherever I go.

U

to urge on

    to incite to greater effort   *(T/S)*

    She's been *urging me on* to return to school and finish my education.

to use up

    to use all of something   *(T/S)*

    The typists have *used up all the letterhead stationery* again. I don't know how they *use it up* so fast. We always seem to be ordering more.

V

to vote down

    to reject by vote   *(T/S)*

    There were several proposals on the ballot for capital expenditures, but the people *voted them all down*.

to vote in

    to elect to office by vote   *(T/S)*

    The people *voted in a new representative* last year, but now that they've *voted her in*, they're not too pleased with the way she's doing her job.

to vote out

    to remove from office by vote   *(T/S)*

    He won by a big margin in the last election, but he's afraid the people will *vote him out* at the next election.

W

to wait on/upon
to serve (T/I)
They don't have enough sales people in this store to *wait on all the customers.*

to wait up (for)
to stay awake (for) (I/I) (T/I)
My parents *wait up for us* whenever we go out. They often *wait up* until midnight or later.

to wake up
(1) *to awaken* (I/I)
I *wake up* every morning when it begins to get light. I can't sleep late any more, even on the weekend.

(2) *to awaken someone else* (T/S)
I asked her to *wake me up* at eight o'clock, but she forgot, so I slept right through the time I was supposed to report for my new job.

to walk off with
(1) *to obtain by excellence* (T/I)
She's such a good scholar that she *walked off with all the prizes* that her school gives at graduation.

(2) *to obtain by stealing* (T/I)
Somebody's *walked off with my good pen.* You can't leave anything on your desk around here without having someone come along and take it.

to walk out
to go on strike (I/I)
The workers are going to *walk out* tomorrow. They took a strike vote last night, but management hasn't made any new offers.

to walk out on

    to leave or to separate from someone suddenly or abruptly
    (T/I)

I don't know who *walked out on whom*. She says that she left him, but he claims that he was the one who *walked out on her*.

to wander around

    to walk or roam without any destination   *(I/I or T/I)*

I like to *wander around the market* and look at all the things they're selling. You never can tell what wonderful bargains you may find when you just *wander around*.

to wander away/off

    to leave for an uncertain destination   *(I/I)*

The children *wandered away*. I don't know where they've gone to, but we can look for them if you're worried about them.

to ward off

    to repel   *(T/S)*

A lot of people think they can *ward off bad luck* by knocking on a piece of wood, but that's just a superstition. It doesn't do anything to *ward it off*.

to warm over

    to warm again   *(T/S)*

I'm going to *warm over the stew* we had last night. It'll taste even better when I *warm it over*.

to warm up

    (1) *to become warm*   *(I/I)*

The weather report says it's going to *warm up* over the weekend. I'm afraid it may get too hot for us to do much of anything.

    (2) *to make warm*   *(T/S)*

Let's *warm up the leftovers* from the party. If we *warm them up*, we can put together quite a good meal.

to warn off

to give notice to keep away (T/S)

We've put up signs to *warn off trespassers* from the power station. If we don't *warn them off*, they could get killed on the high voltage lines.

to wash down

to follow something to eat with something to drink

(T/S)

That was a good steak, and now I'm going to *wash it down* with this excellent red wine.

to wash off

to wash the outside (T/S)

The doors of the kitchen cabinets look awfully dirty. I'd better *wash them off* today.

to wash out

to wash the inside (T/S)

Be careful when you *wash out this pan*. It has a special coating on it that will be damaged if you don't *wash it out* gently.

to wash up

to wash (I/I)

If you want to *wash up* before dinner, there's a bathroom at the top of the stairs.

to watch out

to be careful (I/I)

You have to *watch out* when you cross a street. You have to look both ways to make sure that no cars are coming.

to water down

to weaken, to dilute (T/S)

He was angry when he saw how much the editor had *watered down his story*. She had *watered it down* by taking out anything that might make anyone angry.

to wave back

(1) *to return another person's wave* (I/I)

I waved goodbye to her, and she *waved back* as she stepped into the plane.

(2) *to make a waving signal to go back*   *(T/S)*

The crowd was pressing toward the entrance gates, but the police *waved them back.*

to wave on

to make a waving signal to go forward   *(T/S)*

I would never have had the accident if I hadn't thought that the officer was *waving me on.*

to wear away

to make something disappear gradually   *(T/S)*

The waves are *wearing away the beach* a little at a time. If they *wear it away* altogether, we won't be able to swim there anymore.

to wear down

to make fade or disappear   *(T/S)*

She's sure she'll *wear down my resistance* to giving her a promotion. She's sure she can *wear it down* by doing such a good job over a period of time that I'll have to promote her.

to wear off

to fade, to diminish   *(I/I)*

The effects of the last economic slump have just begun to *wear off,* but now they're predicting another.

to wear out

(1) *to exhaust*   *(T/S)*

The children are so active that they *wear out their baby-sitter.* They *wear me out,* too. After I've taken care of them, I have to take a long nap in a dark room.

(2) *to use or to be used until no longer usable*

          (I/I or T/S)

This fabric will never *wear out.* You can't *wear it out* even if you use it every day for a hundred years. It will still look like new.

to weed out

to remove undesirable items   *(T/S)*

They're *weeding out the members* of the staff who don't contribute to the operation. After they've *weeded them out,* they'll have only topnotch people in the organization.

to while away

to pass time (T/S)

I have to *while away a few hours* before the plane leaves. Can you suggest a pleasant way to *while them away?*

to win out (over)

to win in spite of competition (I/I) (T/I)

She always *wins out.* It doesn't matter how many people are competing against her, she *wins out over all of them* in the end.

to win over

to win to one's side (T/S)

He needs to *win over as many supporters* as he can if he's going to get elected. He's trying to *win them over* by promising anything and everything.

to win through

to win or succeed in spite of difficulty (I/I)

Things seem difficult now, but I'm sure you'll *win through* to better times if you just persevere.

to wind up

(1) *to tighten a spring, etc.* (T/S)

Don't forget to *wind up the clock* tonight. If you don't *wind it up,* it'll begin to lose time.

(2) *to finish, to complete, to conclude* (T/S)

He's trying to *wind up all the outstanding business.* After he *winds it up,* he's going to retire.

to wink at

to ignore, to overlook (T/I)

The supervisors just *wink at us* when we take extra time off. They pretend they haven't noticed anything.

to wipe off

to remove from the surface by wiping or rubbing

(T/S)

I can't *wipe off this stain* from the table. I'm going to need a chemical to *wipe it off.*

to wipe out
(1) *to remove from the interior by wiping or rubbing*
(T/S)
You can get the dirt out of these dishes if you *wipe them out* with a damp cloth.

(2) *to make disappear, to remove without a trace* (T/S)
This economic slump has *wiped out all our profits*. We didn't expect it would *wipe them out* to this extent, and now we'll have to borrow money to stay in business.

(3) *to ruin financially* (T/S)
The last recession *wiped him out* completely. He hasn't got a penny left.

to work off
to get rid of something by work (T/S)
I weighed about ten pounds too much, but I *worked off the extra weight* by exercising every day. It certainly wasn't easy to *work it off*.

to work out
(1) *to be resolved* (I/I)
Don't worry about your problems. They're not that serious — they'll all *work out* in the long run.

(2) *to exercise* (I/I)
He goes to a health club every day to *work out* with weights. He's a real believer in physical fitness.

(3) *to solve* (T/S)
I've made a mistake in balancing my checking account. Do you think you can help me *work it out?*

(4) *to produce a result by work* (T/S)
She hasn't *worked out all the details* in her proposal. As soon as she's *worked them out*, she'll show it to you.

to work up
to prepare (T/S)
Our lawyer is *working up the case*. We'll decide whether or not to take it to court after she's *worked it up*.

to wrap up

(1) *to dress in warm clothes* *(I/I)*
It's very cold out today. You should *wrap up* if you're going anywhere.

(2) *to wrap, to enclose in paper, etc.* *(T/S)*
I've been *wrapping up packages* all morning. After I've finished *wrapping them up*, I'll take them to the post office.

to wring out

to remove something by a wringing or twisting motion
(T/S)
You can use this paper towel again if you *wring it out* and let it dry.

to write down

to put in writing *(T/S)*
They had a secretary at the meeting who *wrote down everything* that they said. They wanted to *write it all down* so they could refer to it later.

to write off

to cancel, to offset *(T/S)*
When you prepare your tax returns, you can *write off any bad debts.* That is, you can take a deduction for money that is owed to you which you are unlikely to receive. It will reduce your taxes to *write the debts off.*

to write out

to write in full *(T/S)*
You can't just assume that people will understand your report if you leave out a lot of the details. You have to *write everything out.*

to write up

to prepare a report, to report on *(T/S)*
She isn't going to be able to attend the meeting, so she's asked me to *write it up* for her. She wants me to *write up a summary* of what everyone said.

POST OFFICE

I've been *wrapping up packages* all morning. After I've finished *wrapping them up*, I'll take them to the post office.

y

to yield up

to reveal (T/I)

The excavation where the archeologists have been working has *yielded up some important information* about life in ancient times.